The Narrow Path
to *Enlightenment*

The Jesus Perspective

Rev. Anna Grace

BALBOA.
PRESS
A DIVISION OF HAY HOUSE

Balboa Press books may be ordered through booksellers or by contacting:

Balboa Press
A Division of Hay House
1663 Liberty Drive
Bloomington, IN 47403
www.balboapress.com
1 (877) 407-4847

Print information available on the last page.

ISBN: 978-1-9822-0188-3 (sc)
ISBN: 978-1-9822-0189-0 (e)

Balboa Press rev. date: 04/06/2018

Scripture taken from the King James Version of the Bible.

Contents

Preface

As I begin this endeavor, I find myself sitting here wondering how it is that I am about to write another book related to the topic of religion. Already, I have penned numerous short stories and essays related to religion, the bible, the devil, and Jesus. What more could I possibly have to share on this subject? What do I need to say that I haven't already said?

And suddenly it dawns on me. The world needs to know. *Religion* needs to know. The people who participate in religion desperately need to know the information that I am privy to. I must find a way to enlighten not the world, but the *religious* world, about the hidden truths I have discovered regarding the road to enlightenment.

The religion I have the most knowledge of is Christianity. There are about 2.2 billion self-proclaiming Christians, and most of them have a wonderful well rounded grasp of the principles of their religion and the Bible. However, Jesus, the most beloved and iconic member of this religion once said that only a few will find the narrow path. This is why I write. If I were to walk into any Christian church on a Sunday morning, all the parishioners I find there are going to hope and pray that they are on the narrow path, and that they have found the truth.

This, however, according to Jesus, is highly unlikely as he states that few find the way. The road to the truth is not common knowledge, and most of those folks sitting in those pews could be in for a big surprise when all is said and done.

The narrow path Jesus speaks about leads to enlightenment,

which includes eternal peace and harmony. Jesus professed that he was the light of the world. He was one of the few who had found the light of the truth. If many in Christianity knew of the truth that will be disclosed in these pages, the world, particularly the religious world, would quite literally be a different place.

The new information I disclose here, if studied and contemplated deeply, can change a person's heart, mind, and soul. The Bible states that renewing one's mind can lead to a completely life-altering transformation (Romans 12:2, *Authorized King James Version*). Thus, this text is written for the multitude of souls that can be changed, transformed, and enlightened by the wisdom herein. It is ultimately for truth that I embark on this adventure to disclose the rarely trodden path to enlightenment. Enlightenment is the answer to ending almost all pain and suffering, at least on an individual level. To all who are looking to improve their thoughts, change their hearts for goodness, discover true joy and peace, and find an unshakable hope in mankind, this is the story for you. For this, I write.

I began my pilgrimage into religion when I became a born-again Christian in early 2010. Previous to that, I had been raised in the Roman Catholic Church, though admittedly we were not very devout. I was baptized as an infant, attended catechism all through elementary and secondary school, and was confirmed in the faith as a teenager. My family didn't attend church religiously, though we were sure to be there on the holidays and a few ordinary Sundays here and there.

In 2009, I started to question God and seek for answers due to a minor but chronic illness. I had a need to know, a deep desire to figure out who God was, if he was real, and what I meant to him. I turned to the internet of all places. I was researching various stories about Jesus and religious experiences. Suddenly, I was caught up, as if in a whirlwind, with a religious experience of my own.

Many people don't understand what the "born again" experience is. Let me briefly explain: It is a supernatural experience where one is supernaturally made aware of information. This information is not obtained through the five carnal senses, but through a sixth sense.

The day that I had my supernatural experience, I received what I can only call a download of knowledge. Somehow, I was suddenly cognizant of the fact that Christ was real. I felt as if I could "see" him in front of me. Though my physical eyes were not truly looking at anything other than the fireplace in my living room, I felt I could see Jesus standing before me. I was aware of a realm beyond this world that was so good and holy. I was also aware of a realm beyond this world that was dark and evil. I was suddenly impressed to follow those Ten Commandments that I had learned about so long ago in my catechism classes. I felt an impulse to read my bible, and I had an undeniable urge to pray and communicate with the spirit.

A myriad of emotions tends to accompany this experience. For instance, I felt tremendous joy, but I also felt guilt. Looking back, I feel that joy was due to knowing that there was something mystical but real out there in the heavens. The guilt that filled my heart was on behalf of knowing that I was not good or holy, and that I could do better as a person.

From that moment on, I became a passionate, faithful and devoted Christian. I read the entirety of the Bible in nine weeks. I began to pray every morning and every evening. I had an overwhelming love for everything "God". I stopped participating in activities which I felt would not please God, and set out to learn which activities would please him. I became a charitable person and a servant to my religion and my community.

I wanted to absorb all I could about the Bible. Ironically, I did not rely on a church to teach me the ways of Jesus. Instead, I felt that I could read and pray and study and God would teach me everything I needed to know, independent of any other teacher, preacher, or pastor. In order to acquire the knowledge I was looking for, I read the Bible and prayed faithfully every day. This was a pattern I would follow diligently for the next five years.

I studied, read, analyzed, researched, took notes and memorized verse after verse for two to three hours a day, in addition to my every morning and every night prayer routine, for at least six days per week. I was determined to find the truth of God and the Bible. I had such a deep thirst to know. Nothing was going to stop me from figuring out all the mysteries and all the secrets of this religious, of the Bible, of Christ, of God, of spirit, and of truth. It became my mission to know everything written and unwritten.

I hope that it is needless to say that what I discovered through all of this research is shocking. In all my hours studying history, Greek and Hebrew, and life as a whole through the Bible, I was astounded at the conclusion. I am scribing these pages now because what I learned is stunning and completely unexpected. And I tell you truly, relatively few people in this world are aware of this knowledge. I guarantee that what I disclose will be new to you, especially if you are religious (or even some sort of mild believer), and it will be utterly surprising. In fact, once the realization sets in that a couple billion people believe one way, but should believe another way, the world will be seen in a different and brilliant light. This light is the light of enlightenment.

If so much of the world believes in one truth but should be believing in another, then a whole population of people is living a lie. Basing our lives on false principles causes much suffering. This book will expose the multitude of lies we have unwittingly believed in, and the truth we should ultimately be believing in. And as one wise person once said, "The truth will set you free." For the sake of our beloved souls and minds, and for the sake of the truth, stay tuned to find enlightenment and be set free.

Chapter 1

The Journey Home

• • • •

Enlightenment. The mysterious, magical, elusive knowledge that humanity has sought for many ages. Gurus, mystics, sages, wizards, philosophers, and scholars alike have boldly plundered the depths of existence seeking for the truth of God and the meaning of life. Though few have claimed to discover this hidden wisdom, those who have can attest to profound transformative peace once it is attained.

The process of finding this veiled and ancient information has been described in tales that traverse all myths, legends, nations, peoples, and tongues. Every society in all eras has endeavored to demystify this special insight into the knowledge of the gods.

Finding enlightenment is often likened to journeying to a wondrous and serene paradise. Each culture has conjured its own unique fable to tease the imagination of the delicacies and delights of this idyllic utopian destination. Though the garden of paradise is rumored to exist, the trail leading to it has largely been forgotten due to its difficult passage and lack of travelers. The path to this heavenly land is known for obscurity and treachery. With many obstacles, trials, and even monsters along the way, few dare to attempt the course. The Bible states that a cherub with a flaming sword guards the gates to this mystical place of peace and abundance (Gen 3:24).

These myths and legends are parables which symbolically depict spiritual and mystical things through representation in the physical world. For instance, the Garden of Eden is supposed to be a physical place. Its exact location, however, is ambiguous or transitory, for it has never been pinpointed on the map. Heaven, too, is supposed to be a physical place, but then again, Jesus once claimed that the kingdom of God is within the human body (Luke 17:21).

The allusions to this paradise are portrayed throughout the ages in all sorts of types and varieties, and it's been called by a myriad of titles such as Nirvana, Valhalla, or Elysium. As we will soon find out, this Promised Land is not in a literal area on earth nor in the heavens, but a locale within the human.

The philosopher's stone, the pearl of wisdom, and the white stone in the forehead all whisper of the idea of enlightenment. Each requires a strenuous, arduous journey in order to be able to finally snatch this treasure from the clutches of fire-breathing beasts. In the Bible, this venture is represented in many areas, but particularly in the story of Jesus' death. Jesus spends three dark days in the belly of the earth to rescue lost souls from the devil and return with the power of resurrection. Resurrection is symbolically the same event as awakening in enlightenment, for it is at that moment that we shall "know in full" (1 Cor 13:12).

In Isaiah 26 and Daniel 12, the condition of being prior to enlightenment is described as death or sleep. Finally, when our knowledge is increased at our resurrection, we are awakened from our sleep, or our deaths in the dust of the earth. Verse 19 in Isaiah 26 reads, "Thy dead men shall live, together with my dead body shall they arise. Awake and sing, ye that dwell in the dust." Daniel mirrors the same sentiment in verses 2 and 4, "And many of them that sleep in the dust of the earth shall awake,...But thou, O Daniel, shut up the words, and seal the book, even to the time of the end: many shall run to and fro, and knowledge shall be increased."

All of these narratives are attempting to expound in a cryptic manner the journey that humans can aspire to undertake toward a true understanding of life. Once the legends are deciphered, a coded message comes through. This message is that which the wisest men to have ever lived have tried to explain for the rest of us. Unfortunately, this journey is one that each man must walk for himself, and he simply cannot be taught this deepest wisdom by another. One must live and experience firsthand this journey to enlightenment, in order for it to be assimilated into *knowing*.

The message of those who have traveled through the deep and murky rivers of the mind to find the pearl of truth goes like this: To obtain a peaceful existence and discover the meaning of life, one must first purify, cleanse and renew their thinking. Removing old beliefs and discrediting the foundational principles upon which one has always stood, equates to a fiery trial in dark and dangerous territory. Lighting upon true wisdom and founding one's beliefs on the new truths learned on the path to enlightenment, rewires the mind. This allows for a total transformation of the person. The Bible states, "be ye transformed by the renewing of the mind" (Rom 12:2). Renewing the mind is the act of enlightenment. Finding ultimate truth is similar to discovering a new and glorious world.

Enlightenment is defined by dictionary.com as 'to give intellectual or spiritual light to; instruct; impart knowledge to, or to free from ignorance, prejudice, or superstition.' *To free from ignorance* is the phrase I want to focus on first. If someone is ignorant, they are lacking knowledge or have misguided knowledge about a subject or many subjects. The way to enlighten therefore is to give truth and dispel lie, or shed light upon. To be enlightened is to learn something completely novel and unexpected. As Daniel J. Boorstin once said regarding true learning and enlightenment, "Education is learning something you didn't even know you didn't know."

To free from prejudice is another definition of enlightenment. We may not believe we are prejudice people. However, every assessment or judgment we make in our minds is a type of prejudice. If we judge something as bad, we have a prejudice against it. We are assessing that thing as substandard due to preconceived beliefs, concepts and principles we have learned in life. After all, in the garden, God said that everything he created was good, very good, in fact (Genesis 1:31). We will discover why we judge things negatively, and therefore with prejudice, despite this affirmation that everything is supposed to be good.

I want to prepare you, then. In order to reveal how we are in the dark, we will have to embark on a deep examination into the reality of our daily existence. We are boarding the train to the abyss of human thought in order to scrutinize the foundations upon which we stand in this world. First, one has to understand what we are believing in, and so we will investigate how we function as a society. Secondly, we will have to find the errors and prejudices that we live with on a daily basis, and determine how the system we operate within is based on a multitude of incorrect assumptions. Finally, we will reveal the truth of how society should actually flow and cooperate, and uncover the true principles we should live by. Many of the scriptures in the Bible will contribute to our new understanding, but Jesus' hidden and unknown teachings will be divulged to bring us what religion and the common standard teachings of the Bible never could - enlightenment.

We will tunnel our way through the deepest recesses of philosophy to reason with a new perspective and draw novel conclusions. In the revelation of new truth is the glory of security, peace, acceptance, and love, all of which contribute to our spiritual well-being. These virtues define the promise of the paradise man has been pursuing for millennia. And it will feel like home when we arrive to that glistening garden.

This will be a profound undertaking and will require some contemplation on your part. As stated earlier, one cannot be taught this experience on an intellectual level, but he can follow sign posts to help release prejudices and shed light on error. If a person has a genuine longing to understand and devotes time to pondering some of the principles discussed along this winding and twisting trail, he or she or anyone can change their thinking. Reading these alternate angles on reality can plant a seed that will eventually grow into an eccentric and startling philosophy – The Truth.

By the end of our journey, if we have completed what we set out to do, we shall have conquered the dragon who guards the gate to Eden. We courageously will invade his lair, tearing down structures, frameworks, and falsehoods in order to unearth his precious golden nugget of knowledge. By the time we emerge at the surface, we should be enlightened, and we shall be free from ignorance and prejudice. We will also grow spiritually by learning new truths and releasing our negative perspectives, as 'to enlighten' also means *to give spiritual light*.

Sometimes the narrow path to enlightenment is a long, confusing, painful journey. Through the analysis of your own deep beliefs, it will feel as if you are being poked, prodded, and certainly offended in many instances in this book. This is a necessary process, as you must realize that what you believe to be true now is not what you are going to be believe to be true by the end of our travels. I am hoping to give you a shortcut up the winding staircase to the Promised Land, but be forewarned. This is not something to take lightly, and the destination is well worth the effort.

The principles of religion will be our blueprint, as religion is the vehicle I chose when I began my travels to the dark underworld. Religion is the system created specifically for the purpose of hunting for the buried treasure of transcendent knowledge. Religion can guide a person to truth, making him or her free from ignorance and prejudice and giving him spiritual wisdom, but few ever make it past the ritual and practice of the standard beliefs of religion. As Jesus once declared that straight is the gate, narrow is the path, and few there be that find it - "it" being ultimate truth. Fortunately, after years of research and study, I have ultimately traversed that skinny path, and the way is now known so that we won't get stuck in the trenches. The map of religion is going to take us into a dry arid desert first, but we should return to a lush and fertile paradise soon thereafter. The garden we will return to is our first estate, our place of origin, and our true hometown.

5

Chapter 2

The Platform of the World

● ● ● ●

As we embark on our journey, we stand upon the train platform, watching the world rush by. Commuters, travelers, various passenger cars, hobos, conductors, and diverse populations gather to launch on their individual adventures. We intermingle with all persons and things on a physical level, in a manner that is very familiar and comfortable. The spiritual level, though, we often neglect to contemplate. What is the force pulling the strings beyond the physical realm, and how are we predispositioned to interact behind the curtain? That which is invisible backstage is what we ultimately want to explore, for the invisible is the true foundation for our daily lives.

One may hardly stop to think about the principles and belief systems that our world is founded on. One may think there are many different beliefs operating behind the scenes in different countries, cultures, and traditions. However, when we examine closely the root ideas of society, we find just a few common themes underneath the structures and foundations of the world.

In every country, state, and community on the earth, each individual is subject to rules and governance. This is one of the grandest similarities binding all peoples of all nations together with a universal belief. Though we may not believe that we have consciously consented to being ruled over by a government, we subconsciously agree to this state of being, or the system would be different by now.

At the dawn of civilization, perhaps in the area of Ancient Babylonia, it was people coming together and agreeing to live by a certain set of rules and standards that allowed for the first community to function and become a society. Before this time, man wandered only in small groups of family or tribe and did not have to establish a formal set of rules that were legislated through a central and common government. It is government indeed that facilitates civilization as we know it.

Mankind has framed together a set of rules to govern groups of people who desire to live within close proximity with each other. Presumably, these laws dictate certain acceptable social behaviors appropriate for public common areas, laws regarding fair trade among the people, laws regarding treatment of aliens who come into the area, a myriad of punishments for those who break laws, a set of officials to implement law, a set of judges to interpret and legislate these laws, and the statutes go on and on and on. All governments operate under these same basic principles. Of course there are slight variations. For instance, some nations have a one man ruling party, while others rely on a jury of peers to judge, but both systems are still structured very similarly in principle.

Civilization is substantiated upon the foundation that obedience to law or government makes man able to live in a community together. Societies who were bound together by obedience to similar laws and principles then drew bounded or limited areas within which groups of people agree to follow the same set of laws. Boundaries of cities or nations therefore spring up around groups of people who are following the same set of laws. From the premises of limited areas bound together through legal concord arises the entity of sovereign and separate national governments.

Laws have the power to affect our behavior, making us more civilized. Laws also have the power to bind a nation together, for whomever will not abide by the rules of a government, cannot be part of that nation or group. All the world operates in this manner.

The government's main role in acting as Supreme Authority is to legislate, execute, and enforce the rules of their society. We, by living under this government, fashion our lives around the expectation of our governing legal systems. We do not steal because it is against the law of our community. We avoid cheating on our taxes because it is against the law of our country. We abstain, for instance, from playing our music too loudly after 10pm because our neighborhoods have curfew regulations, etc. We, therefore, find ourselves practicing certain rituals and behaving in certain ways to please our highest authority.

The guidelines and rules of our highest authority have molded our behavior in the physical world in order that we are able to fit into our society and conform to its etiquette. We can transfer this same practice to the rules and proper demeanor for our workplace, our family hierarchy, our fantasy football league. Everything we do is structured around the foundation of rules, expectations for behaviors, ordinances on acceptable conduct, etc. Our lives are based upon several layers of rules, behavioral rituals, and more rules. Rules are imposed by authority, no matter where that authority comes from. And we simply side step here and jump through hoops there in order to conform and comply with these rules without hardly thinking twice about it.

There are laws and standards for all aspects of our lives. For instance, if we always try to wear the most fashionable clothing to fit in, we are following the expectations and rules of our peer group. If it is fashionable to roll up our pants, this a ritual we practice in order to conform to and keep the rules of the fashion gods.

A Governing Authority is the platform for our entire society. The train station we are present at includes a foundation which is structured by laws and standards imposed by authority. Trying to be obedient to certain rules and expectations effects our physical behaviors. This is easy to understand. On a deeper level, though, and what is of utmost importance, is what occurs when it comes to our invisible belief systems. The existence of government and our subjection to it, influences not just our behaviors, *but our thoughts and beliefs also.*

All of us are guilty of making judgments against or for others because of the laws or standards we hold within our belief systems. For instance, if we wholeheartedly and vehemently agree with the law in North Carolina that states that bingo games cannot last longer than five hours, but our neighbors across the way have had multiple games that go well beyond that five hour limit and long into the night, we would most likely begin to form an unfavorable thought about those neighbors. Suddenly, those neighbors are seen in a negative light. Because the law states there is a five hour limit on bingo games, but our neighbors break that law, we are now forming adverse thoughts and beliefs about those neighbors. They are law-breakers, disrespectful, criminal, audacious, and substandard. Whether we are consciously aware of it or not, laws affect our thoughts and beliefs on a very deep and profound level.

Take note in your mind now. How do you feel when someone cannot live up to societal standards and rules? Do you believe poorly about person who does not conform to the laws of fashion? Do you have a negative opinion of a person who does not abide by societal norms and so lives outside of the boundaries of community standards? It is the law of the land that allows your thoughts about a person to form in one way or another. In this way, we expect people to behave in one way to avoid illegal (or substandard) behaviors, and we develop our belief systems based on those behaviors.

There are just a few reasons for the establishment of government and law. Governments keep us safe and secure from enemies. Governments enforce laws on individuals to keep us safe from one another. These are the assumptions that lie hidden underneath the physical implementation of law and government. Law/government exists due to a foundation which implies that we need to be restricted in carnal behaviors. If there were no law against thievery, for example, many of us would be thieves. We need law to restrain us from acting criminally. The existence of law/government also assumes that we need protection from people in other countries or communities. If there were no laws against bad behaviors, our neighbors may harm us.

In summation, governments and laws exist because we believe humans are not trustworthy. They have a tendency to act disorderly and have the propensity to take advantage of or harm others. Thus, the governing authority must implement rules to guard us from others who may want to hurt us. This is a deeply ingrained inference upon which we agree to stand. The assumption behind the existence of government is a thought process that states humans are innately mischievous, and the prevailing disposition is for people to mistreat one another or behave barbarically.

As a consequence of this premise, we agree to authorize an outside institution to rectify the injustices that individual people (or countries run by people) will commit against others.

Though we assume that running society by fixing a standard of rules and legal limitations for each person to live by is a good way to live, we are going to analyze that assumption. Our communities are full of pain and suffering and hardship. In a perfect world, we would be free from these adversities and we would live instead in harmony and peace. This is one of the places where we need to shed light upon the error of our ways, and to find a better solution for how to structure our societies and lives. The platform upon which we live now, as subjects to governing authority and laws, is not the best or truest way to secure us our most ideal existence - just take a look around. Trying to obey laws and forming governments to enforce those laws has not brought us peace.

What if the presumption of inherent malicious intent is therefore incorrect? What if laws and governments don't stifle bad behavior but justify it? Could the platform the world is built upon be faulty? Perhaps there are deep cracks in the beliefs and principles upon which our world is built. It seems that being obedient to rules has not created safety and security, but a dystopia of sorts instead.

Is it possible that humans are not inborn with a tendency toward evil? Is it feasible that our systems not only allow for flaws in behavior but create them? Instead of deterring and an individual's bad behaviors, could ruling authorities and their laws be the cause of them? Instead of minimizing the world's conflicts could boundaries and limitations of law increase them?

To enlighten ourselves about the foundations upon which the world stands, we will examine these questions and our form of governance. The vehicle we are going to use to analyze these principles will be religion, as religion was created as a way to explore our invisible belief systems.

Chapter 3

Religion: The Vehicle of Enlightenment?

* * * *

In this physical realm, religion is a way to define and understand the requirements of the Supreme Authority, God. To make this venture ever more difficult, most people have an incorrect idea about religion from the start. So we must begin with defining and analyzing the idea of religion itself before we can endeavor on a journey through religion to the place of enlightenment.

At a glance, there are many different types of religion. However, just as all governments are based on similar principles, so are most religions based on similar structures. There are a few religions that fall into similar categories, though they may call their gods by different names. The religion I will be focusing on is Christianity, but because Islam and Judaism are based on similar foundations, we may be able to include these religions in the discussion. All three tend to have some comparable ideas and stand on related principles.

Religion began in an effort to explore that which we do not see. Though people can intuitively feel a force from behind the scenes in the spiritual, we are oblivious to what this essence consists of. Religion was created as a practice to connect oneself with the elusive power beyond, to respect it, honor it, acknowledge it, and acquaint oneself with the ethereal which exists outside of the physical. Mankind had a desire to know this immaterial entity which came to be known as God or the Gods or Nature or Source to feel the presence of this power, and to understand what gives faculty for life itself.

This searching to understand and to connect to God very quickly turned into a physical practice of dance, song, acts or rituals, which are all forms of behavior modification. Humanity was grasping at a spiritual essence and trying to interpret it through physical means. This is perfectly acceptable behavior, for man uses his physical senses to make sense of the world. However, because the essence of God is a spiritual thing, the power of God is diminished in trying to manipulate his entire being to fit into the physical plane. The practice of seeking God became a physical set of rules and rituals, and religion was born. Religion is a very difficult way to actually connect with God because God is spiritual and religion interprets through physical. First, we will inspect the physical aspect of religion, as all we have known at this point is that which we experience through our five senses.

For our intents and purposes, religion was developed when a devout and chosen man spoke with God about God's rules and regulations. Moses, in the Bible, was that particular elected official. He was taken up to speak with God on the mountain called Sinai. There, God gave Moses a set of rules to live by. From these 613 ordinances and statutes, Moses set up a way of life for his community that would continually please God, properly serve him, and constantly acknowledge his rules. Moses became the authority over the Israelites by way of his rules, which dictated his religion and ultimately an entire way of life.

The Bible is one of the most comprehensive documents we have detailing an ancient archetype for this kind of authoritative rule by a supreme entity. Moses' religious and civil community both were established by a higher authority's laws and expectations. Of course, it could be possible that Moses' structure was simply mimicking the bureaucracies which were contemporary of his time or even the preceding bureaucracies. Egypt, for example, had a society that was run by certain rules, rites, and rituals through a central government. The government was ultimately led by Pharaoh. Pharaoh was worshipped as a deity, and rightfully so as he was Supreme Ruler. Their God ran their government by rules and legislation. Whoever rules the land with ultimate authority is ultimately a God by definition. In similar manner, God operated the government over the Israelites through Moses and other selected priests.

If one is a religious person, he or she is living his life with the rules and requirements of God in the forefront of his mind, or perhaps in the back of his mind, depending. This person fashions his or her life around his obligation to God's ways. He may serve in his community to fulfill one of God's requirements. He may abstain from certain practices in order to stay in the graces of God. He may donate money to prove his devotion to God, etc.

The rules of God create a religion which people live by. Religion is simply a set of guidelines, rites and rituals as devised by skilled and pious authoritative or religion persons who have studied and practiced the ways of God. And these rules effect one's beliefs and faith. All the world is governed by a higher authority's laws and expectations, whether that be God or Government. By proxy, then, all people everywhere are practicing the same principles as the system of religion as we all live under Supreme Rule and modify our behavior to stay within the limits of the rules.

Religion is based on the exact same principle as government. If it is acceptable to God to be charitable, I will serve and give money weekly. It is frowned upon by God to have premarital sex, so I will abstain from that behavior. It is unacceptable by God's laws to worship false deities, and so I will avoid those who practice Satanism. I will avoid certain things and sacrifice others in order to comport myself in an appropriate way. Our mannerisms and habits and beliefs simply depend on who we pay homage to and whose rules we are trying to obey: country, community, peers, family, employers, or

God - it's all the same practice in principle. This is the religion we practice in our physical lives.

Consequently, whoever's rules we follow can be called our gods, for they have authority over our decisions and the manner in which we conduct ourselves. This may seem to border on blasphemy, but we must understand the meaning of God if we are to understand religion and government. In the Christian religion, God is one who directs our behaviors and beliefs through rules which create ideologies. We have many different authorities in our lives who dictate that behavior and thought, though, not just the Supreme God (i.e. our governments affect us in the same manner).

In the religions that stem from the Middle East, God manages his faithful constituents by rules and regulations, service and sacrifice, and for their obedience, they are offered the opportunity to reside in a peaceful paradise.

The word religion, in its etymology (the origin of the word) comes from the root *lig*. *Lig* shares a common root with the word *leg*al or *leg*islation. Both roots, *lig* and *leg*, mean law. Re*lig*ion is simply a set of rules or laws to keep for God. And *leg*islation is a set of rules to keep for country. The deeper root of the stem *lig* or *leg* is "to bind together". This is how a community or group is made, bound together by agreeing to adhere to a specified set of rules. I am Christian because I follow this set of regulations. I am American because I agree to live under the law of the land.

This root word *lig* is recognized in the word *lig*ament which simply means bands that bind your muscles to your bones. Religion defined, then, is a group bound together by following similar legislation. This is the definition of country also, or community, or ethnicity, or association, etc.

On the level of the macrocosm, government guides the behaviors and thoughts and beliefs of all peoples. In the microcosm, religion guides the behaviors and thoughts and beliefs of many peoples. Religion and governments are not unique. In order to belong to any group, one must conform to that group's rules and beliefs.

As already discussed, however, we are not living in peace and safety in this world, though both our religion and our government promise this outcome. Our behaviors and beliefs are not based on the best principles, and the evidence of this is that we are not living in a harmonious society. We are holding on to error in the foundations of our structured society and religion, and we need to discover that faulty framework if we are to become enlightened. This spirit behind our misinformed beliefs will be investigated carefully in the next chapter.

Chapter 4

Cracks in Our Foundation

• • • •

Let's remember our train station. Look around now and take note that all of these characters here have one thing in common. Every one of them stands on the same platform in the world, of a higher authority delegating expectations and guidelines and ordinances to rule over us, keep us in check, bind us together in society, and protect us from each other. We all live the religion of life every day. Rules and expectations guide, mold and shape our behaviors, thoughts, and beliefs. We generally agree that this is a decent method upon which to structure our society and protect us from harm. Contrastingly, our theory is going to stand upon the idea that there are inherent faults in this structure, regrettably, that cause us more hardship and pain than peace and security.

Unfortunately, several obstacles arise with establishing the foundation of society or religion upon laws and expectations. This became conspicuously apparent in the travesty that was the Israelites. They struggled for many years trying to obey God and live by his ways, though they seemed to fall short time and time again. Put into slavery twice, fighting a multitude of wars, drinking of bitter waters, and all of them (but two) died before entering the Promised Land and obtaining that peaceful, harmonious reward.

A problem develops when individuals live by someone else's regulations and standards. By definition a person living under another's rule is not a free person. True freedom is defined by having no restrictions, no rules, and the liberty to do as the person feels is correct for his own happiness.

Laws give ultimate authority to another over each individual. Most of us don't mind this so much, as we easily adhere to our community's rules, and it is not a difficult task for most to remain law-abiding citizens. However, when we examine the consequences of being obedient to another's rules, it will be glaringly obvious how the system of legislation itself causes a myriad of complications and predicaments. The religion of life has the whole world in quite a limited, and therefore desperate, state.

In fact, obedience to law is the cause for most of the pain and suffering in the world. That's a big claim to make, but once explained thoroughly, the truth of that is undeniable. Remember we are believing that living with this type of societal or religious structure is good. To be enlightened we are going to pinpoint the error in that thinking and replace that error with truth. Through learning the truth, we will be able to reconcile in our minds why societies and religions have so many conflicts and problems today.

We structure our daily behaviors around rules and expectations of society so that we can fit in, appear somewhat normal, and succeed socially. We use these rules to help us navigate life in this world. Even if our heart is telling us to do some things differently, we sometimes ignore our heart so that we can abide by societal standards. Even if our hearts tell us to stand out from the crowd and be a beacon of uniqueness and singularity by not conforming to a certain regulation, we would have consequences to pay if that action meant we had to break a rule. And so we abstain from expressing our own individual truths and follow legislation instead. Therefore, we often might live in a way that is against what we truly feel or believe in our hearts in order to conform and be obedient.

A simple example of having to agree to a situation contrary to what we believe (because of laws imposed by a higher authority) is outlined in one such circumstance as follows. At the end of the year 2017, there was a nationally known case of a young lady who had been taken as a teenager into a sex trafficking organization. She was sold to a man and held captive by him for many horrific months. She ended up killing this man in order to escape. She was subsequently sentenced to 51 years in jail for this man's murder. Our hearts feel this is an injustice as the woman was experiencing a living hell, and so of course, when the opportunity came to escape by any means necessary, she did so. But, by law, she must serve her term in another prison for an even longer period of time. She now transfers from one hell to the next, and most would agree that this crime does not deserve such a harsh sentence.

There are probably thousands of instances where laws do no justice to our hearts true beliefs and contradict justice. On a lighter note, Idaho state law makes it illegal for a man to give his sweetheart a box of candy (with some weight restrictions). No one can attest to believing that there should be a rule against giving candy, and yet we now have to negate our true desires about giving candy in order to be obedient to this rule. If we want to be law-abiding, we have to conform. We are now limited in what we can choose.

We have just touched upon a couple of problems of living under law. Laws restrict freedom of choice, and relinquish some rights and individual power to another authority. We sometimes must live according to law, even if the truth of our heart is telling us to live another way. Negating the heart's desire to conform to someone else's standards is not a wise nor pleasant way to live. These are all negative side effects of living under another's rule.

There are other dire consequences of living by the laws and expectations of a higher authority which are life altering. Here is one of them: laws create prejudice in our belief systems. The foundational principle upon which our governments and religions are based create prejudice. I am claiming that laws and rules don't just promote or add to prejudice and discrimination, but *create* them. Laws and rules are the reason for prejudice. However, as stated earlier, to enlighten means to free from prejudice. By definition then, if laws create prejudice, *laws help to keep us ignorant.* This is something to contemplate.

If we were to take a look around the train station, we would notice colors, sounds, things that we have an affinity for, things that are unpleasant. The act of observing and assessing with our five senses is the act of judging. We are judging by our own standards, society's regulations, and maybe our religion's guidelines. Judging is accomplished only by the preconceived prejudices that are already programmed into our minds by learned standards, laws, and rules.

In essence, a law, by definition, has to be judged. To declare a judgment is to be prejudiced by the standard of the law. We all live under law, laws results in expectations in behavior, and we judge others by those expectations.

If a person breaks a law or does not conform to standards and rules whether individual or communal, they are judged. This is the nature of law. If a law applies, it has to be judged upon in order to be valid and practical. If a judgment is not made upon the law, it is not a law at all. Judging is the act of prejudice, or as defined by the dictionary, 'pronouncing an opinion and appraising something critically' which is the same act as prejudice which is defined as 'unfavorable opinion or feeling about another group.'

Prejudice is also defined as 'an unfavorable opinion or feeling formed beforehand or without knowledge, thought, or reason.' Here is another definition from dictionary.com, 'unreasonable feelings, opinions, or attitudes, especially of a hostile nature, regarding an ethnic, racial, social, or religious group.' It's a very grave matter then to propose that law is the cause of all of these things. The following details the process by which laws create personal and social prejudice.

Everyone who does not uphold the laws is doomed to the pronounced opinion of "criminal". If you break a law, you are deemed a criminal by definition. *Crim*inals, who are judged critically and whom people have a negative opinion of, are dis*crim*inated against.

Discrimination means to have the power to make judgments, or unfair treatment of a person, racial group, minority, etc.; action based on prejudice. This is the same definition, and thereby, the same action as being prejudice. In religion, the criminal is called a sinner.

Discrimination is also described as something that serves to differentiate. Law, therefore, is also divisive as it serves to differentiate. Those who uphold the laws are judged favorably. Those who break the laws are judged unfavorably. We suddenly have two groups in society. Those who uphold the law and those who don't follow those expectations. Discrimination is the next step for the criminal, as the law breaking population has stepped outside the norm and has not conformed to the agreement society has made to follow certain standards.

Now we have a disparate society. The law-abiding look upon the criminals as substandard, because they are literally that. *Sub* meaning below or under and *standard* meaning and I quote the dictionary again 'a rule or principle that is used as a basis for judgment.' This is discrimination. Albeit, one might consider it a good practice to judge and discriminate by law, it is not so. There is no form of good discrimination on the spiritual level, and we'll find why this is immoral later.

What happens as a result of this discrimination? By definition, we have unfavorable feelings or opinions, especially of a hostile nature, against that population who doesn't abide by the same set of standards as we do. This is a huge problem once it is understood that we are not only talking about criminals as people who break governmental law, but those criminals who break workplace rules, school statutes, public etiquette, or even fashion standards.

Rules bind groups together in cliques, but also keep others out by discrimination. We have agreed to live under the statutes and ordinances of our community in order to be part of that community. If our religion has a rule stating one must show up for church on Monday, but a person is constantly the only parishioner showing up on Tuesday, that person not part of that religious community are they?

If our yoga group has a rule that we must buzz cut our hair and wear purple pants, but we show up with dreadlocks and red pants, we are not conforming to the requirement of the group, so we will soon find ourselves an outsider, not a participant. We are now a living example that the group is prejudice against people who wear red pants. And we simply can't play if we don't follow the same rules because we are substandard. Those who do follow those rules fit in, and they are part of the group.

Another problem with the implementation of law is that a group of legislators must be appointed to limit the allowances on behavior for each group, each government, and each religion. A ruling class is born to decide how society must conform, what is appropriate, and what is not acceptable. This class of lawyers and judges must be assigned so that the society and/or religion is monitored regarding the requirements needed to comply with the laws that they put in place. The Israelites relied on Moses and the High Priest Aaron to help direct the people to be obedient to the statutes ordained in the law. The responsibility of maintaining all stipulations and commandments became a monumental task for Moses and Aaron, and so priests and judges were assigned to share this responsibility. Moses and Aaron and their governors were the ruling class, the sect of society which have authority over the legislation. Our government officials are the ruling class of today.

In order to qualify for the position of judge or "ruler," one needs to know intimately all the practices of social law, and likewise to be a priest, one has to know intimately the practices of religious rite. Suddenly a hierarchy is formed. There are constituents now who are allowed to legislate law or minister unto God, and receive the special benefits and exemptions of the priesthood/government. The managers of the law have special power and privilege and rights because they manage the law and rule by the rules. Law assigns power.

In choosing a special tribe to ordain law, a royal class is created. Royal means regal and the word regal is directly derived from the word regulate and "regulations" – regulation being another word for laws. Therefore, law demands a regal and royal court. Now we have added yet another caste to the mix to further divide society into three parts: the Royals, the Normals, and the Substandards.

Judges have a tremendous amount of power above the norm as they can declare a person guilty, even if the person's action was intended for good and not for harm. Though not common, this type of abuse of power has been seen in all stages of legislation of law. Not only can the execution of law by lawmakers be unfair, but the enforcement of law by police officials can certainly be skewed also. The system is prejudice to its own standards, regardless of individual intention or situation.

What is accepted as perfectly good and proper in some areas is deemed criminal in another. In Denver it is unlawful to lend your vacuum cleaner to your next-door neighbor. Loving your neighbor as yourself is good enough for Jesus, but in Denver it makes one a criminal! In Lexington, Kentucky, it's illegal to carry an ice cream cone in your pocket. Now this may be just plain silly, but it certainly shouldn't be unlawful. What's more, would the man who was found with an ice cream cone in his pocket actually be charged with a crime or fined? Not one person breaking these laws is actually intending harm in their hearts. They are most likely wonderful, loving, giving, ordinary people. Yet, they could be incarcerated, fined, punished, and indicted just like a regular criminal. And someone presiding over the law, as supreme ruler, as God, has decided that these are proper rules.

We are all subject to a higher authority who is more powerful than us. We all have a god ruling over us who may be legal, but not necessarily moral. We are also tied to our community by the rules we agree to follow. We are limited in behavior to conform to acts that are legal and normal. We are strapped into our social group and chained by our obligations to be obedient. And don't venture off the tracks, because you are limited in what you can do, how you can act, even to the point of ignoring the good intentions of your heart.

We are all guilty of believing in and agreeing with this system. There is an insurmountable crack in the structure of our system, for the system itself is based on false assumptions. It has promised us peace, safety, and harmony, but has flourished in separating and discriminating, binding and oppressing, and allowing for conditions upon our acceptance of others.

All aboard as we enter the train car. Buckle on the seatbelt named Law as we exit the station. Unfortunately, this train is heading toward darkness by riding the rails of corrupted principles. Though we think being obedient to authoritative laws will land us in the Promised Land, never has the legal binding of obedience to law delivered us to a harmonious society. It's time to depart the station before it crumbles. I hope your restraints are secure, because we're in for one bumpy ride.

Chapter 5

The Tunnel of Darkness

●　●　●　●

This is the lot we have ended up with. We have chosen the train car called LIFE by governance, even if it is by default. We are bound securely by the limitations of law. Though we consciously don't think that government rule is so terrible, and we believe that most rules are good, proper, and reasonable, the principles upon which those laws operate are backwards. It may be hard to conceive of that at this point, but our train car is about to derail into a deep chasm of servitude and bondage.

This will be your home for the duration of the journey. Our specific car is labeled as Law-Abiding American, Very Religious, and of the Middle Class. These labels were chosen by the conductors as they observed our group to conform to those standards.

If we agree to stay aboard this particular car in LIFE, we will be bound. Once the legally binding agreement is accepted, the direct result is a manipulation of behaviors and actions in order that our particular contract is upheld. Social adaptations are implemented so that one can live within the boundaries of the limits of these aforementioned labels. And thus, a whole lifestyle is also born, simply by the implementation of agreed upon rules of certain societies and certain religions. We must now conform. We must change. We must limit our choices to the expectations of these labels.

Of course, the highest authority of our train car is the God, the Conductor, and the Supreme Ruler of the land. We adhere to his laws as if they are of the highest authority. Does the conductor have the right to act as God at the top of the hierarchical structure of our carriage? The answer is a resounding YES. Apparently we have given them this right, because we all agree together to live in this section of the train for this journey.

Because we have grown up knowing nothing more than this way of LIFE since a very young age, we have found it to be somewhat to very acceptable. We have experienced the laws of religion and the American way of LIFE as a relatively decent living to this point. But what if law were actually a hindrance in LIFE?

Here is the tale of our first hand practical experience with the train car called LIFE.

In our experience, we very quickly and very diligently began to follow along the rails that are pleasing to God, for we are very religious here. Remember, however, that religion is a very broad term as we all live some sort of religion every day of our lives, religious or not. No matter how specific this particular example is, everyone can relate in some manner by their own affiliation with any number of groups or associations. We are also American, so we live to be in the good graces of the governing authority in our community.

We know it is not acceptable by the standard of the Bible to participate in certain activities, nor to behave in certain ways. Consequently, we adjust our behaviors to conform to the expectations of our religion.

We begin a regimen of study, prayer and service to God. We are rapidly conforming to the image of the holy and righteous servant that is the standard for a godly group. We have made silent agreements, promises to ourselves and God that we will obey his ways, and he in return is then to allow us into the Promised Land someday.

This is indeed an unspoken legally binding contract of sorts between the passengers and our God. We are now bound on the narrow path to serve and sacrifice and behave, and God, if he is to uphold his end of the contract, is then to allow us into Heaven at our time of death. We all determine this to be a pretty fair contract, and so this is the rule we live by.

By the time we are a couple years deep on this track of religion, we have completely squeezed and pulled and pushed ourselves to fit into the image of perfect and holy people. We do everything by the Book (the Bible, which is our constitution), follow all the practices, rituals, and rules, upholding our ends of the legal contract, and we are determined to faithfully continue this way of life until our dying breath. We have given up so many things to be able to conform to the ideal and perfect servant.

Though we are the picture of righteousness, we still sometimes feel as though we are not measuring up. Looming over our heads is a constant doubt that we may be doing something wrong or that we are forgetting a rule here or there. Are we good enough? Are we faithful enough? Would we be forgiven when someone lets their tongue slip and curses, taking God's name in vain? What about service for God? Should we be giving more? Is all of our action truly worth enough for an almighty, all holy, perfect, and Great God?

There are so many rules to live by. There is so much service to do. God seems to have more rules and expectations than even our own country's government, and so every time we venture to relax a little, we feel as if we may be breaking one standard or another. Some of us question if wearing makeup is okay, for there is that verse in the Bible about eye makeup being portrayed in a negative light. Others wonder if we should be wearing head coverings, as there is a scripture that depicts this act in a positive light. We're finding that the list of do's and don'ts could go on and on forever.

There are a multitude of religious groups that appear even more pious and more regimented than we. Just how far do we need to shift and conform and sacrifice for God's rules to be acceptable?

The whole of our group decides to abstain from certain holidays that most of the other cars celebrate, because God said in the Old Testament that his designated Holy Days were going to be a statute forever with his people. We decide to honor those holidays as ordained in the Bible, such as Passover and Yom Kippur because we are part of God's special people, are we not? We give up Christmas and Easter with our families because those celebrations are not found in the rule book. It's hard to imagine sitting isolated in our little car on Christmas day as the rest of our families and friends are merrily celebrating together, but that we do for several years.

Our ritual of prayer and study every morning for several hours has us chained. Whether we are terribly busy and strained for time, or even on vacation for a few days, we still feel obligated to study and pray religiously.

Because of our great commission to win people over to this religion and way of life, we speak often about the Bible and Jesus and salvation. This earns us much scorn from unbelieving peers and acquaintances and many rude comments even from family members. After all, we don't follow their lax lifestyle, and so we are outsiders to them.

And what of those people who are not encapsulated in a car designated as religious? Well, in our opinions those others are simply lost, in trouble, and/or living risky lifestyles by not honoring the Most High God. We all know that our conductor is the true conductor and pity the others who do not recognize this. Without religion and without accepting God, the outsiders are lacking holiness, full of sin, and persuaded by devilish influences. Though we feel for them and give charity to them, we know that the Bible says their souls could be in trouble. Though we try to teach them of Jesus, if they won't see the error of their ways, we must abstain from contact with them, lest their uncleanliness rubs off on us. In this way, we become more and more isolated, divided by standards, prejudice by law, and discriminating by ritual.

It should come as no surprise by now that our lives seems to be taking a turn for the worse, as we have already determined that following all of these rules and laws does not work. Law causes division, law causes bondage, law causes discrimination. Law calls for special privilege for some, but subjugation and limitation for others.

We cannot deny either that some of the rules we are obeying cannot be justified by our own moral standards. How does the law of honoring the Sabbath day make me a better person? Saturday was to be set aside to honor God, study his word, stay inside and not intermingle with outside influences, unless it were regarding God's work. We were already practicing this type of abstinence every day of our lives, and now we had to give up even more on Saturday? How are we judged as morally or ethically inferior if we don't keep holy the Sabbath day?

When examined critically, one begins to wonder how there can be so many different practices all stemming from the same God. As we look at the other passenger cars, we see others labeled very religious, though they have chosen other ways in which to honor their God. For instance, in Christianity, just about all of the denominations believe in the Bible, but just about none of them follow the Bible in the same way. One faction worships the saints, one thinks that is illegal. Another group speaks in tongues, another thinks that practice is of the devil. After years of living with these dichotomies, our heads are spinning.

We find ourselves under a legally binding contract that is just about killing us and leaves us worse yet, questioning our conscience. You see, we had (though not verbally) made an agreement in our hearts and minds to follow God's ways when we boarded the train of the very religious way of LIFE. This was a legally binding commitment. If we kept our end of the contract, God would be obligated to keep his. His end of the contract was to allow all of us into Heaven on that final day. Striving to keep our end of the bargain is getting the best of us.

Soon, though not soon enough, it is evident that we are living a life of bondage, sacrificing normal daily activities and time and effort and even friendships to remain as obedient (and therefore holy) as possible, according to the rules.

There are at least three religions that have a rule book from God. The Jews follow the Torah (which translated means Law) and the writings of their prophets. The Christians follow the Bible, which is a combination of the Torah, the prophets, and The New Testament. The Muslims follow the Quran which is a compilation of words of Muhammad as given by the Archangel Gabriel.

Each and every verse of these above-mentioned books and scriptures is a law in itself for the very strict believers. The adherents of these religions believe that these writings are the works of God. Therefore, if something is stated in scripture, it *must* be truth. Law is defined in the dictionary as a 'revelation from God.' Each and every word is revealed by God, and therefore, is believed as absolute law. Scripture cannot be broken because it is the direct word of God. Every word is a law to many believers.

The Bible, therefore, is a book of law (as are the constitutions of governments as they are also written by the supreme rulers of the land.) One would think that God's laws would work, and each and every one of us, if we followed this law, would find fulfillment, peace, and harmony. In fact, this exact sentiment *is* the law of the Bible. God said to Moses and the Israelites that if they followed his words, his commands, and his ways, as written in his book of the law, he would give to them a land flowing with milk and honey. Hence, they would have a harmonious society and peace of mind in a beautiful land. This is the legally binding covenant our little car had also been trying to follow all along, obedience to law in exchange for peace. Yet, in performing these rites and rituals, we are feeling as servants to this religion, sacrificing everything, but still not giving or doing enough nor finding one ounce of peace. Instead, we found ourselves a little fearful of punishment, exhausted by our way of life, discriminating, isolated, a bit nervous about Judgment Day and what would be pronounced at the end of all this.

Of course, that is how law works. In this legally binding agreement, this religion, this way of life, if one of the hundreds of rules of holiness are broken, there are consequences to be suffered.

This fearful aspect of religion is mirrored in the fear of civil law in our daily lives. Our government has promised us peace and safety, but we don't live in that environment in reality. We still fear criminals. We still carefully maneuver through our communities to avoid being mugged, raped, or worse, and we teach our kids the same fear. If we drive a little too fast, we fear we will be pulled over, interrogated, and fined. If we aren't hip to the newest fashion, we may walk in fear of ridicule. If we don't conform to the normalcy of societal expectations, we run the risk of being labeled a weirdo or being ostracized by our peers, and that is often punishment enough. All this, and we still fear our neighbors not only on a physical level, but in the spiritual also. Their ungodliness could influence us if we intermingle too long.

To walk under law is to walk in fear of breaking the law, even if we break it unwittingly. Perhaps I didn't know there was a law against carrying an ice cream cone in my pocket, so I stuffed my double scoop cookie dough sugar cone into my pants. I have just become a criminal appropriated for the wrath and punishment of the judge. Law is a fear based way to try to make people behave and draw out their prejudices and suspicions. This is a very real fear, considering the passengers on the car of LIFE believe every verse and every word of The Book to be the inerrant word of God.

Could this life of servitude and sacrifice and fearfully walking the tightrope truly be what God had intended when he gave humanity his rules and his words to live by? Surely God does not make mistakes and must have intended for good, peace, and safety when defining, legislating, and enforcing his law. He certainly meant for his law to bring peace and happiness to the obedient follower of his law. How is it, then, that one can find himself so worried and limited by this law and still walking in fear? And now our governments mirror the exact structure with similar results.

For example, we all have to earn money somehow. We all have to toil the field and strive faithfully to bring in the fruits of our labors. We all have to tithe by paying our taxes. We all have to sacrifice time, effort, sweat, tears in order to be appropriate for the scrutiny of societal standards or religious standards.

It has taken us a long time realize that our train had taken a detour into a deep dark tunnel of confusion, fear, bondage, and servitude. This way of LIFE was supposed to offer us happiness in the Promised Land, a peaceful, secure and safe land flowing with delights, milk, honey, etc. It seems that though we are holding tightly to our end of the bargain, it is not delivering on its promises.

Chapter 6

Rounding the Bend

• • • •

In my religious journey, I was absolutely certain that it was not in my interpretation of the rules nor my practice of the rules that was in error. I was striving, studying, toiling, and serving consistently, faithfully, religiously. I knew of no one person in my community or family who knew the scripture like I did, who prayed as diligently as I did, and who sacrificed their time like I did in an effort to be sure to follow the rules correctly. I was even sure that my piety could rival that of the priests or pastors or preachers in my community. That is how dedicated I was.

Finally, one day, I sat back from my prayer with a realization. I was not lacking in my performance to my legally binding contract. I was upholding my end of the agreement. I was accomplishing everything humanly possible. And that is when lightning struck with a couple of revelations. First, it was the system of law that was futile, biased, and ineffective, not my practice of it. Secondly, a mere mortal human *cannot* perform the works of this contract, and that is why a Savior needed to come and fulfill it for us, thereby freeing us from it.

A light turned on that magical moment, and it is a light that continually grows and expands with joy and harmony to this day.

The switch had been flipped, and I had made it through the narrow path to enlightenment. After years of diligent study, my brain lit up my mind had been renewed, and I was completely transformed from that moment on. To many fanatic Bible believers, this may not seem like such a profound revelation. It's the information that this discovery led to that is revolutionary.

First, I would ask you to think deeply upon your own religious beliefs and practices to determine if you can relate to this scenario. What I had been practicing for five long years on the very religious train was the Old Covenant of Moses. Now don't get me wrong, I lived for Jesus and thought I understood Jesus and memorized Jesus' every word and action. But I was practicing the Old Covenant, the Old Law, the Old Contract. The Old Covenant of Moses from the Old Testament was my religion and my life.

The Old Legally Binding Covenant states that if a person will follow the rules as outlined in the scripture and if he will be obedient and serve faithfully, he can earn his lot in the safe and secure Promised Land. Many of us in Christianity follow the Commandments. At least the Ten. Most of us try to follow God's ways, his voice, knowing when to abstain from certain activities so that we can please him. Some of us read the scriptures daily. Christians serve God faithfully by attending service or performing acts of service in our community. We tithe by offering money or charity to organizations for God. We offer gifts at the proverbial altar. In trying to convert people to this religion, we in essence offer the harvest of souls. If one does not perform these works as suggested in God's rule book, is one truly a good and faithful servant?

A person is to be performing these works if they are any kind of decent Christian. However, these works are the works of the first and old covenant.

Let us compare Moses' religion which proceeded from the old covenant with God, to the way of life I just adhered to for five years.

1. Service: Moses set up the standard for service to God. He was instructed to build a tabernacle to house all the things

of God so that the priests and practitioners would have a designated place for service or mass. Moses essentially developed the blueprint for service. In principle, I was doing the exact same thing. I was finding a way to serve God at least weekly in my own individual way. And I was a good servant at that.

2. Sacrifice: Moses created the rules and regulations for an elaborate and mass animal sacrifice, which was an essential part of pleasing God. I too was sacrificing my life, for we all know that this body is now to be a living sacrifice for God. Romans 12:1 states, "I beseech you therefore, brethren, by the mercies of God, that ye present your bodies a living sacrifice, holy, acceptable unto God, *which is* your reasonable service." I was now that animal, sacrificing my life to please God. I gave up this and I abstained from that, which means I *sacrificed*. I became that living sacrifice, still alive and yet giving up my life.

3. Tithing: The Israelites were commanded to give one tenth of their wealth to the altar of God. I diligently toiled to give as much as I could, at one point giving 1/10 of my monthly income to charity.

4. Offerings and Oblations at the Altar: I faithfully performed many works so that I could offer something at the hypothetical altar of God. Though there is no longer a Jewish temple on the Temple Mount to physically offer fruit and wheat, but in principle, my offerings were just as hard earned. Daily I offered my prayers, studies, works, writings, and video blogs as an oblation in the name of God.

5. Studying Scripture: No one knew the scriptures like the Priests and Israelites. In fact, rumor states that many Jews had the entire first five chapters of the Torah memorized forwards and backwards, literally. I was approaching this level of zealous study myself.

All of these practices and rituals were outlined in the Old Testament by the agreement of Moses and the Israelites with God. The people were commanded to study God's word, particularly on the Sabbath day. They were the prototype for temple/church service. Their ritualistic animal sacrifice is unparalleled to this day. No one religious group is known to be more pious than an orthodox participant of this religion.

The people of the old contract did these things in order that they could obtain a lot in the Promised Land. This was their legally binding covenant with God. They would obey his laws, serve, sacrifice, tithe, offer, and study, and he, in return, would allow them into the Pearly Gates of the peaceful land flowing with milk and honey. This way of life became their religion. This way of life became my religion. Or should I say this religion became my way of life. Remember, religion means Law. I was bound by this legal contract, this law, to do all of these acts so that in return I could reap my reward at the end.

What is wrong with the old covenant? All of religion still practices these rituals today. We are supposed to be doing these works so that we can be counted worthy, aren't we? Doesn't scripture say that "faith without works is dead?" We are supposed to be sacrificing much, even our lives. Doesn't scripture say, "I die daily" and we must be "crucified with Christ?"

In principle, we are all serving the laws of governments or communities or social groups in the same manner. We all do this to fit in or to appease. In religion, we are to be obedient to be counted worthy of acceptance, as in society. We all obey laws so that those who then enforce the laws can in return offer us peace, security, and safety in our community.

Yet, one glorious day the lightbulb that was ignited in my mind burned with the hypocrisy of all of this. It all fell into place like a missile dropping from an airplane… There is something wrong with my way of life, my religion, even according to scripture. It was causing separation, prejudice against others, a denial of my heart in some cases, and servitude and sacrifice in others.

Doesn't scripture say in Galatians 3:10 that those who are performing "the works of the law are under the curse?" Why was I still trying to meet the requirements of the old law?

Doesn't scripture say in Galatians 4:5 that Jesus came "to redeem them that were under the law?" Why was I acting as if I were not redeemed by Jesus by practicing this law?

Doesn't scripture say in Romans 10:4 that "Jesus Christ is the end of the law for righteousness?" Why was I still trying to be righteous by practicing the works of the law which was to be ended by Christ?

Doesn't scripture say in Colossians 2:14 that Jesus "blotted out the handwriting of ordinances"? Deleting the laws and statutes of Moses and "nailed them to the cross?" Why was I still trying desperately to adhere to all those laws and regulations regarding service, offerings and tithing?

Wasn't Christ the perfect servant? Why am I still trying to serve?

Wasn't Christ the perfect sacrifice? What better did I think I could sacrifice?

Didn't Christ pay the price? Why was I still trying to tithe my way through?

Wasn't Christ the Word made flesh? Why was I still abiding by and memorizing line after line of the written Word?

In principle and in practice, it was as if Christ never came. I was practicing Moses' standard of religion, not Jesus', as does all of Christianity 'til this day. Our governments still practice these same principles of rulership and authority because they do not comprehend Christ's real teachings. The problem with following these ways of the old covenant is that Jesus came to release us from the bondage of that legally binding law and religion, as described in all the verses above.

Though we are rounding the bend in the depths of the tunnel now, our GPS is failing so we proceed cautiously. Still in despair and confusion, I found myself trying to justify my way of life for the past several years. I was questioning why it was that I was feeling so trapped and so limited and so chained to performing all of these good deeds. Religion was supposed to be a joyful communion with God, and to do his work and perform these rituals should be fulfilling and pleasant. I had seen the pious and mild mannered holy folk going about their business with satisfaction and quiet resolution. However, after several years of performing my service, I had grown frustrated with these rites, and that was very troublesome to me. Please apply these sentiments to any governing influence you adhere to also in your train car of LIFE.

Though I had dedicated my life to God, these physical practices were not fulfilling. Instead, they were draining, and sometimes downright grueling. Spiritually, my energy for life felt diminished, for I was pouring my heart and soul into rituals that were a "curse", according to the Bible, and that is exactly how I was feeling.

Of course, I turned to scripture and prayer for answers to this dilemma. What I found was reassuring on the one hand. On the other hand, I was appalled that no one had ever warned me of the truth of this so-called sanctimonious living. For anyone who has ever longed to devote more time and effort to religion, please read the following first.

Scripture teaches that my perspective of suffering and hardship was valid. "For as the sufferings of Christ abound in us (2Co 1:5)... And our hope of you *is* stedfast, knowing, that as ye are partakers of the sufferings (2Co 1:7)... That I may know him, and the power of his resurrection, and the fellowship of his sufferings, being made conformable unto his death (Phl 3:10)... Who now rejoice in my sufferings for you, and fill up that which is behind of the afflictions of Christ in my flesh for his body's sake, which is the church (Col 1:24)......Beloved, think it not strange concerning the fiery trial which is to try you, as though some strange thing happened unto you (1Pe 4:12) But rejoice, inasmuch as ye are partakers of Christ's sufferings (1Pe 4:13)."

Fiery trials of judgment, pain, insecurity, fear, bias, doubt and suffering. This is exactly what my journey in this religion was made of. I was totally relieved in this validation by my comrades, the apostles. I was actually supposed to be working and toiling away, even unto death, according to scripture.

The truth is that I did die. Spiritually, I had died. Scripture validates this point, too. Romans 6:3-4 "Know ye not that so many of us who are baptized into Jesus Christ are baptized into his death? Therefore we are buried with him by baptism into death." I was baptized, and thus dead with Christ. All Christians who are baptized are dead and buried also. This is biblically clear and sound doctrine. Unfortunately, this whole rite of passage was appalling to me. It was at this moment that I realized that religion had lied to me, as has all law. The system of obedience to law has promised something it cannot deliver, love and peace for all individuals. And physical obedience and ritual is not the way to reach peace nor God.

My baptism into Christianity (once as an infant in the Catholic Church, and twice as an adult into the Christian faith) had been celebrated as a splendid and joyous occasion. I believed my baptism into this religion had just gained me entry, like a new birth, into salvation, glory, and eternal life. To learn that scripture, the holy word of God, says the exact opposite about my initiation into this religion was quite an upheaval. I had died instead by baptism and by giving my life to this way of living.

Like Christ then, we are to suffer and die. Here is the allegory we described in the first chapter of our book. The road to enlightenment is to include a renouncing of our old belief patterns, which is likened to a dangerous and tedious journey on a dark and hidden path. This darkness is the sleep of death that is the allegory for ignorance and prejudice in the Bible. Coming into bondage by serving God's laws is not life, but death (ignorance and prejudice). My experience of religion was very intense, but can be transferred on a bigger scale to the macrocosm of anyone living under someone else's rule. It is the belief in governance to provide us with peace and security that needs to be reconsidered, for living in adherence to that belief is bondage and suffering.

Jesus repeatedly suggested we follow him. We have followed him indeed, into the "heart of the earth" (Matt 12:40), which is the pit of darkness and death, where hell is supposed to be located. By giving up my old way of life to serve this religion, of course, symbolically I had died, and this is precisely what the Bible means when it says we sacrifice our lives. In essence, the covenant that God offers us is to provide us eternal life after death, if we sacrifice our lives for him while living.

In an epiphany, it all became so obvious. In my baptism into this religion, I was making a silent covenant with God to follow all of his ways and complete all service by physical works. It was this physical servitude and bondage that was supposed to kill me by vainly striving to reach God and heaven by rite, ritual, song and dance, which ironically does not work.

So the story goes that most in this religion wandered aimlessly in the desert for 40 years without ever reaping the benefits of reaching the paradise where God resides, but instead suffering the consequences outlined in their covenant over and over again. Despite this, the Israelites continued in their servitude until their physical deaths because it is impossible to light upon the true dwelling place of God by physical practices of religion. The Israelites toiled and tried with all their hearts, and they died not only spiritually but physically before entering the Promised Land. Now that narrow path is the same one that Christianity is also on, as they continue with a physical practice of servitude as ordained in the Old Covenant.

I had been in that desert wasteland, offering years of diligent service. Faithfully obeying God's laws and God's commands had not delivered me to the Promised Land either.

A new truth that I discovered is that religion believes it is earning holiness and cleanliness by practicing physically all the rules outlined in the Bible. To serve God is to be holy, we think. To attend church or tithe or do charity work is to be holy, religion claims. This is the same principle the world lives by today. If we obey the law, we will be judged as good, acceptable and a worthy participant in society. If we do all these things, we will live in a paradise on earth. So many billions of people have tried this method throughout the ages to no avail. The pious seem to be failing despite their servitude, but the other participant of this legal contract is not upholding his end of the bargain either. He is supposed to provide us with a safe and harmonious society - the security of the Promised Land, and that just hasn't happened either.

The real truth is that practicing this ritual of obedience and servitude is not justifying anyone in any way in the eyes of God because these religious practices contrastingly foster prejudice, division, and lack of freedom which is the opposite of holiness. Prejudice, which comes only by judgment by law, is the opposite of acceptance and love. Prejudice is the reason for rejection, segregation, negative opinions, all which lead away from peace and harmony. Being prejudice is the opposite of being enlightened, according to the definition of enlightenment.

Prejudice, division, and segregation by physical works are what nurture and develop true criminal behavior. Therefore, criminality is a byproduct of law. People under law are then bound to suffer in judgment: headed for a life in dystopia, doomed to an eternity of imprisonment, servitude, and bondage to the devil in the fires of hell in the afterlife.

Isn't living a life of servitude to this commitment I had made to adhere to this religion already bondage? By following God's law, I indeed was in bondage, which is confirmed in Galatians 4:24, "the one [covenant] from [Moses at Mount] Sinai, which gendereth to bondage."

The Bible confirms my suspicions. Law, practicing this way of life, is death, and entering this religion is death. Hebrews 7:9-11 declares, "For I was alive without the law once, but when the commandments came, sin revived and *I died*. That which was ordained unto life, I found to be unto *death*. For sin, taking occasion by the commandment, deceived me and by it *slew me.*" How I could relate to this scripture, which is describing a spiritual death. All of my practices were keeping me in good shape physically, but spiritually, I was drained by sacrificing my life.

Entering this covenant with God was supposed to bring eternal life, instead I found death. Baptism into this religion is supposed to signify a rebirth, thus the water ritual, but instead, scriptures confirms we enter into death, buried with Christ by baptism. The law *deceived* by revealing what sin or criminality is through prejudice and division, and leading us to believe we need protection from others. Deception is a trick of the serpent. And, worse yet, death is the playground of ignorance.

Death in the Bible is the equivalent of sleep and ignorance. This is the exact opposite of what man created religion for, which was to seek enlightenment, truth, God, and the reason for life. But God is a spiritual being who I was trying to reach through rite and ritual. I became aware that I had to find a way to reach God spiritually.

The Old Way of Moses was not working, and this is why Jesus came to give a New Covenant, the Truth, and the Way. I thought I was believing in Jesus, but was practicing Moses' religion of physical ritual and behavior modification. What most don't realize is that Jesus came to set us free from our bondage - to this religion and to law in general. Jesus came to give us the true Way to the Promised Land through a new covenant. In Romans 7:14, the Bible states that the "law" is supposed to be spiritual.

Chapter 7

Releasing our Bonds and Following the Light

• • • •

With our GPS defunct now, we find ourselves in quite a quandary. Our religion is coming apart at the seams and is ready to derail the tracks. We have no rituals to perform, no service to accomplish, no rules to obey, and no time and effort left to sacrifice because we have realized that these things don't lead to heaven as promised. It's as if all of our years in religion have been futile and have led only to bondage and death, and these ideas are substantiated even by scripture itself. The trip doesn't end in this deep dark tunnel, however. There is a light that shines just around the bend.

It is time to release the restraints of our bondage to daily toiling and striving. We can now unbuckle our seatbelts, for it is time to move about the cabin freely, and to simply trust and have faith that the true Almighty and Powerful God will take us to our destination.

There is a leg of the journey yet to be traveled even after our deaths. God has promised that even if we do pass away, there is a plan for resurrection and life eternal in the Promised Land. We have been obedient unto death, as Jesus was. Next, God should be faithful in resurrecting us. As scripture states in Romans 6:4 "For if we have been planted together in the likeness of his death, we shall also be in the likeness of his resurrection."

And so perhaps our journey will not be in vain. Though the Old Testament religion of servitude, sacrifice, offering, studying and tithing has not earned us passage into the Promised Land, Jesus' profound, mysterious, and hidden teachings will. His teachings are to set us free from the bondage that was included in the physical religion as dictated by laws and commandments previously. Unfortunately, the whole of Christianity is not aware of the enigmatic teachings of Christ, or they would not still be practicing the religious principles set forth by Moses.

Christ taught of the mystical beyond the physical practices of service and sacrifice, which includes knowing God in a spiritual manner. Jesus demonstrated through what is called a "new covenant," that knowing God does not come by behaving well, being subservient to a ruler, nor being obedient to a divisive, flawed, and prejudiced governing body.

Our hope in having done all those deeds and works of religion and sacrificing our lives in doing so, is to now be prepared for resurrection from the death and ignorance that subjection to law has put us in. One must understand that our death has been symbolic and spiritual. Our resurrection will also be spiritual by a renewing of our thoughts and beliefs. We are now to regain a wonderful living in the afterlife if we can learn the truth and the way.

The resurrection brings us to a spiritual paradise that is to be discovered while one is still living, but only after dying symbolically to find it. As foretold in many myths throughout many millennia, we have taken a journey into the dark and deadly underworld to uncover the principles of hell and dystopia. We now understand that the structures and beliefs that our world stands on are causing unrest, prejudice, bondage and ignorance. Now that we have breached the dragon's lair and discovered his lies, we can slay him and ultimately locate his treasure which he has guarded so effectively. It is time now to set our sights on that pearl of wisdom, grasp it with our minds, and trust God to teach us of its life giving and regenerating truths.

As the Light of the World once declared, the Kingdom of Heaven is within the human, and not something found outside of the human. As we begin to approach that new land, we will examine Jesus' philosophy so that we can start to see the paradise through the fog that our old way of thinking has caused. It is time for the truth of Jesus to come in and uphold his end of the bargain, which is to guide us through the clandestine entrance to heaven within.

In the preface of this book, I spoke of astonishing information, and it is in this chapter where that information will begin to be disclosed. It's time to aggressively pick up speed in order that we can comprehend the new information revealed. It is a narrow path, remember, but have faith that we can stay the course with the light that guides us from within.

If we were in bondage by law in our train car, we are set free by having no law. Christ came to fulfill the law (Matt 5:17), end the law (Romans 10:4), and finish the law (John 19:30), so that we indeed could be set free from it. It is only by removing the physical practices that law and religion require that we can begin to see God spiritually. As we detail the principles that Christ taught, please try to choose which faction you belong to. Do you believe in Christ's spiritual teachings, or do you practice a religion which is opposition to Christ?

One reason Jesus came was to set the prisoners free. We should all know what was holding the prisoners captive by this point in the story - law. Law is the only thing that can hold a person in prison. It is bondage to be restricted by the limitations of law. It is also a major undertaking to continually strive and toil to accomplish all of God's commandments in order to be a good servant. In the same manner, it is also a major undertaking to continually strive and toil to uphold all of society's expectations to be accepted. If familiar with the requirements of the Torah, one can clearly imagine the daily struggles of the entire community to live and serve in that extravagant manner. The Israelites were chained to perform all 613 tedious ordinances, and in the same manner I was bound to obey The Ten, and to serve, sacrifice, tithe and offer (as are all Christians). This behavior proves a lack of faith in Christ, however, since he came explicitly to save us all from this legally binding covenant of religion. We can now choose to walk out of the prison, rather than remain in there by choice. Being obedient to religious or civil authority does not earn us a peaceful state of being. Peace must come from within first in order to manifest outwardly and not the other way around.

Col 2:14-15 describes the magnum opus of Christ, "Blotting out the handwriting of ordinances, which were contrary to us and against us, he took them out of the way, nailing them to the cross. Spoiling principalities and powers, he made a shew of them openly, triumphing over them in it." The translation from Olde English to modern language reads like this: Jesus blotted out, erased, deleted, all of the ordinances, the laws, the statutes, and the commandments that are unfortunately still performed from the Old Testament Covenant. The principles which were derived from the law's implementation were contrary to us and against us. He showed that the principles behind those laws were rotten and corrupt by spoiling them. He triumphed over the laws of that very contract at the cross. The whole system is foiled. He was demonstrating that governance by rules places people in a state of ignorance, prejudice, and bondage, though the principle behind the law originally stated it would gain us closeness to God in his garden of delights.

The Son came to fulfill the old covenant so that we don't have to perform it any longer. "Think not that I have come to destroy the law, but to fulfil," states Jesus about the first covenant agreement in Matt 5:17. To fulfill means to satisfy all obligations, to complete. He came to give us a new and better covenant to reach God (Hebrews 8:6). Romans 10:4 declares that Christ is the end of the law (and therefore the end of religion that requires obedience to law and ritual) for everyone who believes. We are not to sacrifice, service, tithe, study, or obey in the new covenant. In reality, there is nothing to obey in the new covenant, even the 10 Commandments, if Christ has deleted the law and commandments. Jesus brought a new command, to love all. Love cannot be commanded and therefore is no law at all.

"For Christ is the end of the law for righteousness to everyone that believeth," states Romans 10:4. Now, by Christ's work, no one can be counted righteousness in God's eyes by doing the works of the law. Performing good works, serving God, serving community, and sacrificing time, money, and effort cannot deem you holy and righteous in God's court. For God has no court without a law to legislate. All are therefore declared innocent and set free from prison.

As these new realities begin to settle in, we can see how the new teachings of Christ are forming a new picture for us. We have to take these novel principles and apply them to our governing systems of today also, which may be more difficult of a task. As we continue to learn, we will proceed with putting the puzzle pieces together.

The second reason Jesus came was to defeat the devil. Now, the devil is the progenitor of all evil, wickedness, and bad behavior. If the devil is defeated, so goes all inherent malicious behaviors, vicious acts, and horrific intentions. At this point, if we look at the world, we may think Jesus has failed in defeating the devil and his works. We will soon begin to comprehend how he indeed accomplished this feat at the cross, and how inherent evil does not exist. Trust and have faith that this will all come together in your mind.

The Christian religion believes they must "put on their armor to fight the wiles of the devil" (Eph 6:11). In fact, those of the Christian religion are the biggest believers in the devil. Today, by the existence of government, we also believe we must fight others, for the government exists to keep us safe from threats of the evil enemy. But, look at the astonishing truth of the matter here. Hebrews 2:14 and 1 John 3:8 talk of the destruction of the devil through Jesus' death. "That through death he [Jesus] might destroy him that had the power of death, that is, the devil;" and "For this purpose the Son of God was manifested, that he might destroy the works of the devil." In both of these passages we see that the devil is already destroyed and defeated through Jesus' death at the cross. We will soon examine how this is true, and how no one in the world today is inherently evil, particularly by the influences of demons or devils.

In a related thought process, the Christian religion believes that the world is full of sin and sinners. On the contrary, scripture states, "sin is not imputed where there is no law" (Romans 5:13). There is now no law by Jesus' work at the cross where he blotted it out, and so there can be no sin, for God has no standard to judge us by any longer. This is how the blood of the lamb washed away the sin of the entire world. If we yet believe in sin, we have no faith in Christ, because sin cannot be imputed when there is no law to define what sin is. There could be no criminals if there were no laws to point out what criminal behavior is.

We begin to understand that a man is not judged by his physical behaviors. If a man cannot sin (because there is no law against any carnal acts), he is not deemed unjust, unworthy, or unholy in the eyes of God. This means that no one is not worthy of God or to be in the presence of God. All are welcome, all are forgiven and all are innocent. There is no law to judge man against, he has free passage through the Pearly Gates. This flows perfectly with the truth of Jesus who stated that the kingdom is within the body. If Heaven is within our bodies, minds, and hearts, who or what could ever deny us entrance?

Secondly, if all are innocent and allowed access to Heaven, is any man truly evil? We know that only goodness is allowed in paradise, and if God accepts every man, we have to start thinking differently about the nature of man. It seems that this theory may hint at the fact that man is not innately wicked, despite how he may behave on the outside. It is well known that Jesus, as an expression of God himself, hung out with sinners, tax collectors, prostitutes and other seemingly unacceptable types. Apparently the idea that God requires cleanliness and perfection by obedience to law is false. Instead, no one is excluded from God's entourage.

Further revolutionary thought comes from Romans 4:15 which states, "For where no law is, there can be no transgression." Only where no laws are can there be no criminals. Only where no laws are can there be no prejudice determined by a person's legal or illegal behaviors. Only where no laws are can there be no discrimination according to someone else's standard. Only where no laws are can there be no bondage, conformity, ruling class to separate and divide. Only where no laws are can all be innocent. If there were no laws causing criminality by faulty principles, there would be no prejudices.

"And he is the propitiation (payment) for our sins, and not for our sins only but for the sins of the whole world," declares 1 John 2:2. We grasp by the teachings of Jesus that man no longer has to live in fear of doing something bad, unholy, or wicked for God accepts all men equally no matter their behavior in the flesh. We know that these truths were portrayed simply by triumphing over the law and the principles upon which that law stood. Those principles were obviously false. God does not judge mankind by obedience to laws and adherence to good behaviors. Thus, the world is set free to do as we please, knowing that God accepts us no matter what because he loves all unconditionally and this is his only command, per the teachings of Christ.

For now, this seems like too much freedom which will lead to complete anarchy. Trust that once we implement the deeper teachings of Jesus, everything will be put in its proper place and order, and peace will reign not chaos. If we get rid of the idea of evil and sin, accepting that no one is substandard by these false ideas, we start to understand that everyone is okay. Love starts to seep in to our hearts.

And so we have arrived, travelers, at a completely new truth. In this world (and in religion), our society is founded on the basic principle which states, "Man needs rules to keep him in order, and those rules need to be enforced by some type of government. Without rules and government, there would be chaos and crime in abundance. Anyone breaking a rule is worthy of punishment or discrimination. A human is naturally a sinner." It turns out each and every one of those statements is backwards and based on lie, according to the philosophy of Jesus. With these falsehoods come a slew, a multitude, a mountain of intertwining mistruths and prejudices.

The lies that relate and connect within our framework for society have to do with the legal system, judges, courtroom trials, punishment and reward, freedom and servitude, highest morality, fairness, acceptance, unconditional love, the character of God, the identity of man in relation to God. All of these related systems come tumbling down like an avalanche upon the foundations which we have stood upon. All of it fails. The crack in the ice has been blown wide open, and not one snowflake can withstand the heat of the truth. This snow covered mountain is a volcano inside, and it is time for eruption.

The road out of the pit of death and back to the surface is harrowing but exhilarating also. In learning what comes in to replace law and the Old Covenant, we will find a revelation to awaken us from the dust, which includes a new truth of God, a new foundation for society, and a new perspective on life. Jesus' teachings will show just how a lack of government can right the wrongs of society. His lessons on unconditional love will exhibit how everyone can change their hearts and mind to be set free from the oppression societal standards have placed upon us. The result is clear thinking, natural behavior and a harmonious peaceful community.

Chapter 8

Spirituality and Conscience; The Hidden Teachings of Jesus

• • • •

I hope by now that you have lost all faith in governing systems of the world, of our communities, of our religions, and even of the judge who presides in your own mind to dole out prejudice and discrimination. I mean that truly. As forewarned, the old systems which you believe in must fail. There is now a new truth we must learn. Hebrews 8:13 says, "In that he saith, a new covenant, he hath made the first old." By this new covenant, mankind is to be set free from their bondage to the very rules of their religion and government and all those rules that bind and limit in society. Jesus' hidden teachings will show us what should replace government and religion and lead the world to a truly harmonious Utopia.

It comes as such a relief to be released from the servitude and sacrifice of practicing religion. Jesus came to help the Israelites out of their covenant with God and to give them a better covenant. Galatians 4:5 says Jesus came to "redeem them that were under law." This scripture declares that it was those under strict civil and religious governance who needed redemption, not anyone else. Matthew 15:24 states, "I am not sent but to the lost sheep of the house of Israel" because Israel was following

Moses' law, and obviously were in need of help. As we know, Christianity has been grafted into the house of Israel (Romans 11), and they too need a Savior now just as much as the Israelites did then. But, then again, so does all the world, as we have all believed in the rule and authority of law and government.

Romans 3:20 states that no one can be justified by performing the works of law. If adhering to the physical rituals of the law (any form of law) is not making mankind justified, it is making us instead unjustified. Doing these deeds is causing our guilt. They are causing us to be criminal by causing bad morality, judgmental hearts, faulty belief systems, and segregation by cliques. If there were no law to impose these principles upon us, there could be none of these erroneous practices. No one can be a criminal if there is no law to act against. "Where no law is, there is no transgression," states Romans 4:15. It sounds as if the Bible is endorsing anarchy here, but let's relearn this concept in the correct context.

We have described the physical practices of our legal structural system and how we change our behavior to abide. This obedience and belief in the principles of the law also influences our thoughts about others. Our goal, however, is to inspect the workings behind the scenes through Jesus' alternative thought processes to come to a new conclusion about the operation of society. Jesus' foundation for societal harmony is based on invisible beliefs and assumptions which we neglect to contemplate. It is only in the investigation into his unseen principles where we can learn a new spiritual truth, for the spirit is defined in the unobservable. Let us take a look at an example which describe what Jesus believes about laws and judgment.

There is an account in John 8 of Jesus going *against* the law of the Old Testament. Yes, Jesus broke the law, regardless of what vocabulary one wants to use to justify Jesus' words and actions in this chapter. What it all boils down to - Jesus broke the law of Jehovah (the God of the Old Testament).

The account goes like this:

> "**3** And the scribes and Pharisees brought unto him a woman taken in adultery; and when they had set her in the midst, **4** they say unto him, Master, this woman was taken in adultery, in the very act. **5** Now Moses in the law commanded us, that such should be stoned: but what sayest thou? **6** This they said, tempting him, that they might have to accuse him. But Jesus stooped down, and with *his* finger wrote on the ground, *as though he heard them not.* **7** So when they continued asking him, he lifted up himself, and said unto them, He that is without sin among you, let him first cast a stone at her. **8** And again he stooped down, and wrote on the ground. **9** And they which heard *it*, being convicted by ***their own* conscience**, went out one by one, beginning at the eldest, *even* unto the last: and Jesus was left alone, and the woman standing in the midst.**10** When Jesus had lifted up himself, and saw none but the woman, he said unto her, Woman, where are those thine accusers? hath no man condemned thee? **11** She said, No man, Lord. And Jesus said unto her, Neither do I condemn thee: go, and sin no more."

Please take a good look at verse 5 above. The law of Moses (as given by God) commanded that this woman should be stoned. Jesus, on the other hand, did not condemn her to death, as the law required. The Pharisees (who are the leaders of the religious sect) when they heard truth from Jesus, and left in shame. It is by law that we sometimes do the wrong things, it is by our heart and conscience that we do the right thing.

In fact, this passage tells us who has the higher authority, authority even over the law of Moses' God. The Pharisees were convicted by *their conscience* to leave the scene. Apparently, their conscience was speaking to them at this point, and it was not stating "death by stoning." This means their conscience was going *against* God's law, as God's law required death by stoning.

First, they wanted to kill this woman according to the law. Jesus helped them to see that their conscience, however, was telling them to release the woman. She did not deserve death for committing adultery. Perhaps her actions were indeed questionable, but she did not deserve a death sentence by stoning. And it was their conscience that revealed the truth of a just judgment. The law, on the other hand, did not reveal a just judgment.

The law was incorrect when trying to determine the highest ethical reasoning. The law was accusing this woman as a criminal, worthy of death. Jesus thought, however, that she was worthy of a second chance, of mercy, of forgiveness.

By the law, the Pharisees were ready to discriminate against the adulterer with a negative opinion of her. They were ready to cast her out as a criminal. In fact, she was so substandard, she would need to die.

Enter Jesus, and now scripture states something new. It states "sin is not imputed where there is no law" (Romans 5:13). In this situation, Jesus defied the law, broke it, and declared the woman forgiven instead of guilty. No sin was imputed upon her, as Jesus was challenging the law of Moses and Jehovah. By listening to a higher authority within, he usurped the written law, and in essence, triumphed over the law that states that an adulterous woman needs be stoned. Scripture says in Col 2:14 and 15 that Jesus, "blotted out the ordinances" and "triumphed over the principalities (principles)." Jesus showed that the principles upon which the law of Jehovah stood were unjust.

Jesus showed the law's prescribed punishment to be invalid for the circumstance. The woman was subsequently set free. The highest court had declared her innocent, the court of the conscience and morality, which has the highest authority in terms of true ethical judgment.

Many Christian religions would like to say that Jesus got rid of ceremonial and sacrificial law only, which is why the Ten Commandments are still taught in every Christian church. I tell you truly this is not correct. Jesus challenged even the Ten Commandments as shown here, as the law against adultery is Commandment number six. "Jesus Christ is the end of the law for righteousness for everyone who believes" (Rom 10:4). He ended all the laws by satisfying every requirement necessary to please the God of the law. If there is no law, no one can be a criminal any longer. Not only that, law is now shown to be the wrong way to righteous. Following law does not make one approved in the eyes of God.

If there is no law to legislate, God is not a judge. Therefore, God is not prejudice. God has no conditions, laws or regulations on his acceptance of any human being. God does not discriminate. We are now allowed into God's group because we can no longer transgress the law, for it does not exist. The notion of sin cannot be validated either, and therefore no one is a sinner.

If God is not a judge, who are we to judge another's behavior? This is for you to consider individually. But know that God does not judge mankind according to man's carnal behaviors nor man's actions. Adultery is not unacceptable, but forgivable. If it is forgivable, was it unacceptable in the first place? Apply this philosophy to any act we have a negative opinion of deep in the back of our minds and hearts.

This was a major revelation for me, as I had believed in the image of a law-giving, judging God for my entire life. God is not a judge. The judge is a false image. The whole world is declared innocent because Jesus blotted out the law, and therefore, no one is able to be judged as substandard. What is the office of God, therefore? There is no prejudice or discrimination in God's eyes, according to the example of Christ.

Rules are not the highest authority in the land. As already

described in previous chapters, some rules are simply unjust, unethical, and unnecessary. If a person breaks one of these rules, is he truly evil and deserving of eternal hellfire or even jail time or any punishment? A person lending his vacuum to his neighbor is not a criminal, and so the law is incorrect and biased by the standards of the law makers. They do not have the authority to determine who to discriminate against, though they act as though they do. In fact the true highest authority wouldn't, doesn't discriminate.

Scripture states directly and indirectly that only a person's conscience can judge the truth of a situation. God has written his truth in our hearts, minds and conscience, says Romans 2:15. In our conscience is where God speaks. Our conscience is the highest authority. Our conscience is God. In our conscience is an intuition which has a connection to the highest truth.

Each and every situation has a different set of circumstances and so a law written in stone cannot judge correctly. For instance, a husband ran off three years ago with another woman to another country. He has not been able to be located, and so a divorce can't be granted to his first wife. By law, the wife is still married but she is now having a relationship with another man. This is still called adultery by Old Testament law, though no one would truly blame this woman for moving on. But it goes even deeper than that, much deeper.

If there were no governing law, there could be no transgression, says scripture. This seems to state that if we had no governing body over us, no one would be acting criminally, badly, wickedly. No one would be committing murder if there were no law against it.

Let me explain. What allows mankind the propensity to misbehave is the fact that mankind follows corrupted external laws which twist a man to act *against* his very nature. For instance, according to Old Testament law, a father or mother would have to stone their child for cursing at them. That very signature which God Almighty programmed into man's conscience has to then be denied. In going against their conscience (which of course tells them not to stone their child to death), they instead perform an evil act by listening to their societal standard, which demands stoning as punishment. It is simply not true that wickedness was their nature, but that they were manipulated by their law. Would anyone truly be guilty if their misbehavior simply comes from an erroneous belief in false principles? ...If their misbehavior simply comes by *ignorance, sleep, a "death" caused by law itself*?

We have already established that law binds us into conformity. It binds the mind and shapes behavior. For instance, for many years it has been believed that homosexuality is against God. Now, people who feel the propensity toward same sex relationships, if they want to be acceptable to God, have to act against their natural intuition in order to conform to societal expectations, which were ordained by God. This causes them to go against their nature, and it is only when a person goes against his nature that he can act unnaturally and commit harm.

And here we come to an ultimate truth of enlightenment. The foundational truth here is that mankind is created in the image of God, and therefore fueled by the very energy of God, which is always good. Man is born innocent and pure, made in the image of goodness. This goodness and moral decency is there within every man by nature in their heart and conscience, for all are made of the essence of God. Intuition is the voice of God. If we were to listen to our God-given intuition, man would always be good.

Remember that the need for law/government is predicated on the assumption that men behave badly so we need to be protected from them, which is the reason for the existence of rules in the first place. The truth, however, states that man is pure and innocent and good by nature. Therefore, we need no protection from one another and no rules to limit our behaviors. We would all be good if given the chance to express our true nature. Due to law, we are obligated to obey and conform to another authority, and we are thereby limited in displaying the internal truth of our hearts, which is naturally good.

If the court system of law were dethroned as the highest authority on morality, the true highest authority could take the throne. The true highest authority is found in our hearts and conscience. The great Albert Einstein said, "A foolish faith in authority is the worst enemy of truth." For many years we have had a faith in the authority of government. This governing authority has unknowingly been our enemy, keeping us ignorant through limitations of law. Law binds our behaviors and our minds so that we can't think truthfully nor can we think outside of the box.

Now, the Bible states that man is no good, no, not one, but this is referring to the fallen state of man. One the contrary, when Adam was made in the garden, scripture states that everything that was made was good, "very good" in fact. The Bible also states in John 1:9 that Christ is the light that lights every man who comes into the world. Christ is good, this light is good. Every man starts out with this good light until they are twisted by societal standards and false principles. It is the belief in erroneous ideas that puts us to sleep or makes us ignorant. And all law that every man lives under is founded on a false assumptions.

Jesus says we don't fight against flesh and blood, but principalities and powers. It is the principles (principalities) we believe in that twist us. We believe that man behaves badly if left without governance. This is a false principle, but one that justifies the need for governmental rule. And thus, the assumption for the way the world is run is false. When we listen to a false authority as our highest authority, it leads to a myriad of problems. We are believing in false standards, which ultimately means we are not believing in truth. This is why Jesus said the truth would set us free.

A person conforms to outside law, and in doing so behaves *against* his nature. Then and only then, humans have the propensity to commit crime. One can only become evil by a twisting of his own mind to go against his nature. We have been manipulated into believing in evil by allowing a governing law to tell us what is right and wrong, good or evil. That existential law now becomes the highest authority in the land, the God of the land. But that existential law can never be as fair and just as the voice inside our conscience.

If the conscience were given its proper governing authority, and we always listened to the conscience, we could never act criminally. Remember, where no law exists to misinform and cause prejudice, there is no transgression. The existence of evil then is due to the obedience to a contorted governing system, which allows one to hold false beliefs and honor corrupt principles. This equals being ignorant and defines unenlightenment.

We now have to know and listen to our true highest authority, our God, and that is God's voice inside our conscience and inside our hearts. Scripture says that God has written his truth on the fleshy tables of our hearts. Listen there for the proper way to behave, think, feel, and don't allow external standards and judgments to persuade otherwise. This practice of acting upon our intuition is a spiritual practice, and if practiced, the pearly gates will open. God will be found.

Because the whole world is under law, we remain somewhat ignorant, and we have an inclination to discriminate and act criminally. What Jesus proposes is to get rid of government to eliminate prejudice and bad behavior, and listen to the True God within regarding moral behavior and societal standards.

We believe, according to the principles behind our false legal systems, in transgression, wrong-doing, sins, criminals, and evil. We believe the government exists to protect us from these negative things. If the government exists, the evil must exist. This is false, for everything in the garden is good. It is simply a belief in erroneous principles that has twisted our minds. Only twisted minds can commit evil. If everyone had a straight mind and was thinking clearly we would not commit evil, for we are good.

What the New Testament proposes is that we erroneously believe in evil, and so it is substance. Hebrews 11:1 states, "Now faith is the substance of things hoped for, the evidence of things not seen."

We have put our faith in a corrupt system, and all that system has substantiated is more corruption.

What the Old Testament proposes is that we have eaten of the knowledge of good and evil, and that is the reason for all the evil in this world.

Chapter 9

Ye Shall be as Gods, Knowing Good and Evil

● ● ● ●

Have you ever heard any pastor preach on the Tree of the Knowledge of Good and Evil? Perhaps you have heard of this general story and the context and circumstances surrounding the tree: the serpent, Eve being deceived, and Adam following Eve's prompting. Have you ever heard disclosed what exactly is contained in the fruit of that tree? I wager the specific fruit of the tree remains a mystery to most.

In the previous chapter, I referred to the fallen state of man and scripture describing that state when suggesting that no man is good. However, when Adam was created in the Garden, everything was very good, including Adam. And then Adam and Eve ate from that tree of which they were tempted by the serpent. "For God doth know that in the day ye eat thereof, then your eyes shall be opened, and ye shall be as gods, knowing good and evil," teased that subtle serpent (Gen 3:5).

What precisely is the Knowledge of Good and Evil? Believe it or not, the Bible tells us exactly what the knowledge of good and evil is. Be prepared to learn a new truth and come another step closer to enlightenment.

The Knowledge of Good and Evil is Law. The law describes

what decent and acceptable behavior is. The law details what is evil and unacceptable behavior. Law dictates, "Do this if you want to be counted holy, law-abiding, and part of the group, good." Law also dictates, "Don't do that evil act if you expect to be counted worthy." "This is good, this is bad." Laws! Law defines and outlines what is good and what is evil in the eyes of the governing authority.

Let that sink in for a moment, because the next statement could be rather disturbing for some. If Law is the Knowledge of Good and Evil, the God that gave the Law in the Old Testament was not God at all, but the serpent, pretending to be God. Don't close the book just yet. This truth is shown time and time again in scripture. In order to renew our thinking, let us see the evidence of this.

Most prominently and directly, scripture reads in black and white that the Law given to Moses is the Knowledge of what is Good and what is Evil. Here it is in context in Deuteronomy 30 verses 10 and 15, "If thou shalt hearken unto the voice of the LORD thy God, to keep his commandments and his statutes which are written in this book of the law...See, I have set before thee this day [in this book of the law] life and *good*, and death and *evil*;"

Secondly, Moses carried a serpent staff, which was very powerful and destructive. Moses' face "grew horns", says scripture. A horned man carrying a serpent staff should give you quite a different image of the esteemed Holy Man of Judaism and Christianity. Here it is in black and white in scripture.

Exodus 4:2-6 states, "And the LORD said unto him, What is that in thine hand? And he said, A rod. And he said, Cast it on the ground. And he cast it on the ground, and it became a serpent; and Moses fled from before it. And the LORD said unto Moses, Put forth thine hand, and take it by the tail. And he put forth his hand, and caught it, and it became a rod in his hand:" This serpent is the renowned and powerful staff Moses.

Exodus 34:29 says, "And it came to pass, when Moses came down from Mount Sinai with the two tables of testimony in Moses' hand, when he came down from the mount, Moses wist not that

the skin of his face **shone*** while he talked with him." According to Strong's Hebrew Concordance H7160 (shone*) means:
to shine

1. (Qal) to send out rays
2. (Hiphil)to display or grow horns, be horned

Definition number two says that in the Hebrew language, the word used in scripture here means 'to grow horns, to be horned.' In piecing this information together, we should be developing an image of the devil here, should we not? Sculptors of the Renaissance, including Michelangelo, sculpted Moses with horns, looking exactly like the image of the devil. This is one character I am not sure I want to trust in the light of conglomerated truth, though I deeply trusted in him for many years.

Next, Jesus called the very religious, very dedicated, law-abiding priests and judges of the Law of Jehovah vipers and serpents, referring to the serpent in the garden. He said to those who were strictly following Moses' and Jehovah's law in John 8:44, "Ye are of your father the devil, and the lusts of your father ye will do." Please take note again that this was spoken by Jesus to the priests and ministers and judges of the Old Testament Law. These holy men were doing nothing more or less than what I had been doing for years, trying to follow the commandments, study scripture, offer, tithe, and sacrifice. Apparently, according to Jesus, this obedience and servitude equates to selling our souls to the devil. Sacrificing one's life for a promise that will never be fulfilled is futile, and a trick used by the devil.

This brings us to the fact that the first covenant was not working. Hebrews 8:7 states, "If the first covenant had been faultless, then should no place have been sought for the second." The promise was that the Israelites would be able to live in a peaceful land if they followed the laws and rules as outlined in the scripture. They have not attained peace to this day, though they have tried for generations to honor their God in every way imaginable. The first covenant is faulty. Can an omniscient God create a faulty system?

The Old Covenant, that which stated "If you follow these rules, I will reward you with a land flowing with milk and honey," was a covenant with spiritual and intellectual death. When the commandments come upon us, we die according to Romans 7:9. The law required diligent servitude, prejudice against others, and strict ritual in order to be accomplished, and it did not and does not lead to heaven. Jesus' new teachings instead were the Way, the Life, the Truth. I was beginning to be certain I did not want to serve the God who requires a sacrifice of our life, our time, our energy, and of our souls.

The God of the Old Testament states in Isaiah 45, "I form the light, I create darkness; I make peace and create evil; I the Lord do all these things." But the New Testament directly contrasts this statement when it says "God is all light and there is no darkness in him at all." It also says in Matt 7:18, "A good tree cannot bring forth evil fruit, neither can a corrupt tree bring forth good fruit." If God is good, he cannot create evil. All the dark things attributed to God through Old Testament stories are simply not talking about the true God.

A good tree could not bring forth the fruit from Numbers 31:17-18 where "God" orders, "Now therefore kill every male among the little ones, and kill every woman that hath known man by lying with him. But all the women children, that have not known a man by lying with him, keep alive for yourselves." One does note here that the Lord is telling them to take female children for the purpose of laying with them. Isaiah 13:18 allows for this behavior, "And I will dash them one against another, even the fathers and the son together, saith the Lord: I will not pity, nor spare, nor have mercy, but destroy them." There are so many verses where the Lord YHVH, Jehovah, Yahweh, God, speaks despicably in regard to concubines, slaves, the murder of children, and slaughter of all kinds. This is not love, but evil, and doesn't our conscience tell us so?

Once again, the Lord spoken of in the Old Testament scriptures cannot be true God, as he is a Lord. Lords are rulers. A Lord needs rules to rule with in order to be a ruler. Jesus' father has no rules, as the Son was able to delete them at the cross.

Jesus was trying to portray an ulterior philosophy when he said my kingdom is not of this world in John 18:36. Jesus may indeed be a King, but, where he comes from Kings don't legislate laws, they set the prisoners free by triumphing over the rules, thereby declaring everyone innocent.

In John 6, the crowd wanted to bring Jesus to Jerusalem and crown him King. Jesus quietly escaped that scenario, because, again he said his Kingdom is not of this world, and he meant it. The crowd knew that the scriptures spoke of a mighty King that would come bringing war and vengeance to destroy the wicked and save Israel. Most were totally oblivious to the fact that Jesus was the prophesied Messiah because they were expecting a King and Ruler and Warlord. Jesus shattered this image acting instead with humility, forgiveness and peace. This is true majesty.

The Bible prophesies of a future judgment day when Warlord Messiah comes to dole out the wrath and vengeance of God in an apocalyptic sequence of events (Revelation 19). The truth is however, that God no longer has anyone to punish or judge, and so this scenario is absolutely fictitious. This Messiah, who is supposed to ride in on a white horse with sword-wielding armies behind him, is not an accurate perception of the true Jesus. Jesus was a prince of peace. Jesus taught to love our enemies, turn the other cheek, and put down the sword. Shall he in the future retract these values, and come to fight? Will he bite his tongue, swallow his words, and admit to being inaccurate in his stand for peace at all costs? Will he declare that we should kill our enemies instead?

His armies are prophesied to be holy, clean, and clothed in white linen to signify their righteousness. The true Jesus, however, hung out with an entourage of sinners, prostitutes, tax collectors, and Samarians (the lowest and dirtiest of all). Does God only associate with the clean who were washed by obedience to law as religion would have us believe? According to the demonstration of Jesus, God keeps company with those who are washed by faith in him, no matter their carnal acts and behaviors, whether bad or good. Holiness and acceptance does not come by obedience to law as the scripture seems to teach.

Isaiah chapter 2 appears to prophesy of a future Messiah who will sit on top of Mount Zion as King, legislating and enforcing the laws of God. "And many people shall go and say, Come ye, and let us go up to the mountain of the LORD, to the house of the God of Jacob; and he will teach us of his ways, and we will walk in his paths: for out of Zion shall go forth the law, and the word of the LORD from Jerusalem." Contrastingly, the actual Messiah deleted the law and triumphed over the principles upon which it stood. Could this image be why the Israelites missed his first coming? They, too, were expecting King Warlord to uphold the rules of Jehovah. In reality, Jesus vetoed and broke the rules of Jehovah as demonstrated by the story of the adulterous woman.

What about the image of the King who stands on the mountain top showered with the adoration of the world? Christianity loves this deity and pictures in their imaginations his shining glory while singing his praises. They serve him and bow to him. Ironically, we already outlined how this regal image does not fit the true character of a Messiah. Erroneous understandings have created a false image of him. Who is this prideful, boasting image that is worshipped in Christianity as Jesus was opposed to this type of demonstration of pride and idolatry? Who is this King who requires relentless servitude and faithful reverence? Jesus instead was humble. Jesus served others. Jesus did not exalt his throne above all others. Instead he knew all were equal, including himself.

Jesus did not dole out wrath upon those who were sinners unlike the God of the Old Testament, but forgave. If truly forgiven, they were never guilty in the first place. Of course, they were not guilty, because there is no law to judge them by.

Jesus came to save us from this law and this religion, and therefore the God who ordained this law and this religion. That subtle serpent came to give us the knowledge of good and evil, the knowledge of the law, and Jesus came to save us from him and his law. The two works he accomplished at the cross were to destroy the devil and to blot out the law. The law and the devil were both the enemy.

I made a statement in the previous chapter that goes like this, "Now, people who feel the propensity toward same sex relationships, if they want to be acceptable by God, have to act against their natural intuition in order to conform to societal expectations, which were ordained by God." Reread this statement as It should be now: "... if they want to be acceptable by God, have to act against their natural intuition (which is the voice of the true God) in order to conform to societal expectations, which were ordained by God." How can acting to be accepted by God make one act against the true God? One of these Gods is obviously false, and according to Jesus, it is not the voice inside the conscience that is false. Instead it is the God of the law who misleads.

The truth is that the Bible has the world believing in one image of God and Son, but the true living flesh Son demonstrated something starkly in opposition to those portrayals. If we choose now to believe in Jesus, we need also question scripture, which has implied false characteristics of the Messiah. We are warned of this antinomy in ideas when scripture paradoxically states that the "letter killeth" speaking of the scripture itself (2 Cor 3:6). If only people would believe in Jesus rather than the letter.

And so one cannot believe in the character as developed in the scripture of God the Father and God the Son, if one were to actually believe in the image of the true Jesus who walked on earth. These two characters are the antithesis of each other. One is true, the other is false.

Now we know why the world is in such as a state. Our highest authority, our governments, our gods, have given us rules to live by.

They have given to us the knowledge of good and evil. The serpent, the devil is the one who holds this fruit in actuality, and so we follow after the governing principles of the "devil!" As the bible confirms, this world is under the "prince of this world" who is also known as the devil. And the world's principles are the same principles as the Old Testament God.

The truth of what is morally decent and ethically correct lives inside of our hearts and our minds, and this is the law we should listen to. It is that guide within us that is supposed to be the supreme ruler, because it is indeed the Supreme Ruler who speaks there.

Chapter 10

The Train of New Thought

• • • •

As we start to head in another direction now from our old understanding, we begin to look to spiritual practices and truths for guidance. We now know that Jesus' path is not discovered through the religion which demands obedience, servitude, and conformity in the physical world. These are outward demonstrations of a physical piety and false relationship with God. Jesus taught that the kingdom of God is within, and the key to finding it is through going within to examine the foundational beliefs upon which we stand. Listening to the heart and the conscience in quiet prayer and meditation is going to open the gates to the Promised Land. Though you have always heard the voice of God within, his voice has been entangled with the imposition of existential influences from the world without.

How do we truly know then what God's intuition is telling us as opposed to what thoughts are being mixed with faulty logic from society? The distinction can become clearer when one realizes that God is love, and this is precisely why he speaks in the heart. That voice becomes easier to understand through the spiritual practice of quiet meditation, prayer, intention to hear and listen, not physical servitude.

1 John 4:8 states, "He that loveth not, knoweth not God; for

God is love." One thing that must be understood is that love, true love, is unconditional. The God of the Old Testament, on the other hand, had conditions upon his love. Conditions are rules upon love, laws upon acceptance. True love, however, is total acceptance. True God loves all unconditionally, no matter what kind of behavior they display in the physical world. Behaving badly is simply a result of not listening to their inner voice, but outer corrupt information.

In putting Jesus' philosophy into practice, we will compare two people. By Jesus' teaching, it is declared that a homosexual person is perfectly made in the image of God, and completely accepted and loved by God, and God made him or her to be homosexual, though the Old Testament taught something different. In keeping with that same doctrine, one might want to argue then that a murderer was created perfectly to be a murderer and is totally accepted by God, regardless of his murdering behaviors. It is true that this killer is accepted by God, but God did not make him to be a murderer. One was made in the image of God and is thinking perfectly clearly inclusive of his homosexual behaviors. The other was also made in the image of God, but took on corrupt beliefs to act murderously. One is different than the other. Here is the explanation.

What is revealed in Jesus' philosophy is that mankind is inherently good and perfect. If he or she has done something that the *heart* and *conscience* tell us is morally incorrect, like murder, the conscience supersedes any written law and so must be right. Murder is wrong. A man or woman does not commit murder because he or she is naturally wicked and evil; for he was created perfectly in the image of goodness. However, he or she has committed an immoral act of murder because his or her naturally pure and perfect conscience was contorted, manipulated, or damaged by existential circumstances, beliefs, principles, judgments, and fears. It is only a twisted psyche that can bring forth glitches in behavior.

Acts of evil then arise through fear and confusion and false beliefs. To state the obvious, a person committing a crime isn't thinking clearly. Remember our premise; the laws that remain today cause conformity through behavioral adaptation, by a manipulation of a person's nature and his mind. He is no longer thinking *naturally*. Unnatural thoughts arise, which leads to criminal behavior.

We have established that the murderer is not intrinsically evil, just ignorant or confused and so behaving wickedly. What about the person who is not so conspicuously malicious, but is practicing a questionable way of life? Homosexuality has been bordering on the outskirts of societal norm for centuries or longer. According to our pure hearts and minds that we are given by God, the homosexual simply cannot be inherently evil, but still possibly may be confused. How do we know if being homosexual is something natural or if his or her psyche has also been twisted, and so homosexuality is actually a glitch in behavior caused by a damaged psyche? We need to determine if the *act* of murder is inherently wrong as most believe, and if the *act* of homosexuality itself is inherently wrong as many believe.

Let's evaluate what our consciousness says about homosexuality and/or murder remaining in a perfect world where no one is manipulated or twisted by incorrect beliefs. Pretend that we can simply blot out the pre-programmed opinions in our minds about homosexuality and murder. Both prejudices against these acts were most likely planted in our subconscious by a remnant of societal beliefs which are aligned with Old Testament principles. Jesus has whited out what was written in the scripture, though the scriptural teaching was tragically embraced by society, and grew into a monstrous discriminatory practice. Erase any notion of bias against either one of these acts, and believe that God has not decreed a judgment on homosexuality or murder either way. This is how we use our moral compass to determine which act if either, homosexuality or homicide, is morally acceptable:

We must ask ourselves, are homosexuals harming anyone by committing homosexual acts in their own homes? Are they creating hate or generating love? Is love of any kind a demonstration of darkness and wickedness, or a demonstration of light and goodness? The truth that is revealed in our conscience today is that homosexuality is acceptable. This act of love is just as acceptable as a heterosexual act of love. Love wins and is eternal, because love is the essence of God, and love does not harm.

(Of course, both heterosexual love and homosexual love can be twisted into an act of darkness. Regardless, both are innately good if coming from a clear and innocent heart. Both can be warped into evil acts by minds that are not thinking clearly, but love is its natural form is always good and from God.)

On the other hand, murder does not remain in a perfect heavenly society, because murder harms. The law of the heart dictates that an act of murder is harmful. Death, hate, fear, and harm do not follow us into the Promised Land because they are against goodness and harmony and love. Harmful acts are done away with but love, love of any kind, remains in our Perfect Society.

And so we have easily been able to make a clear, true, pure decision about the law of homosexuality and the law of murder through trust in our very own hearts and conscience. In forgetting preconceived and programmed judgments, homosexuality equals love and so can remain in the heavenly community because love is our nature. Murder harms and equals darkness and does not exist in the perfect community because harm is against our nature. Only acts of intuition and innocence abide in the land where minds are thinking naturally. This is why enlightenment is so important. It helps us to think naturally through listening to our intuition and blocking out the noise of misleading principles from society.

Does discrimination of any kind remain in a heavenly society? No, discrimination harms and must not remain in a harmonious civilization. That means all carnal laws that create discrimination have to go. Love is the only law here, for this is where the heart reigns. At its core, the heart does not know discrimination, but only love, for that is the only thing written in it by God as that is all God is.

One might argue that someone's conscience might say something different than another person's conscience. Someone may think their conscience says that homosexuality is not love, but an abomination, mirroring the sentiment of the verse in Leviticus 20:13 "If a man also lie with mankind, as he lieth with a woman, both of them have committed an abomination: they shall surely be put to death; their blood *shall be* upon them." Not so. The beautiful thing about Jesus' theory is that the same truth that was programmed into my conscience before my birth was programmed in your conscience before your birth by the one and only Creator. There is only one conscience of which we all partake individually and collectively. And remember, Jesus blotted out all ordinances, including this one in Levitius 20:13. It does not exist any longer.

Therefore, our opinions cannot vary (if we wipe away all preconceived notions and deep rooted societal expectations) on what is acceptable and what is not. That same light and truth that is written in me by nature is written in you, because you and I are made of the same living energy (which is the essence of God.) It's consciousness. If you are conscious, as am I, that consciousness is the living thread which connects all of us on the same communication line with God. Conscience is the great I Am, and all of us have it. It does not vary, but is the absolute truth.

The universe is only made of one substance, *living energy.* Living energy is the true God of this universe, and so every atom declares the same story and the same truth. The living energy is always only for giving out, sharing, expanding and perpetuating energy. It is a fountain of never-ending abundance and supply and the force within is the essence of light and love only.

To find the original and pure truth that was programmed within us through our own life energy, humanity has to erase all of our preconceived principles that we were indoctrinated throughout many centuries to believe. One must go within oneself, for that is where the kingdom of heaven is found. We must examine our souls, our hearts, and look for that light and that love that we are given by our Creator. Here, all biases are eraed and love is unconditional.

One might also argue that men and women would run wild if there were no laws to control them. Not so, for they are inherently good. If there are no prejudices, fears of judgment, and anxieties about the possibility of misbehaving, then our true essence shines through. When a person is thinking correctly, all that is exhibited is love and goodness and kindness. If no one assumes another is a criminal because there are no laws to judge by, then love and peace begin to reign. Where mistrust was once the basis of civilization, trust now becomes the foundation. Where fear of others and fear of rejection was a foundation for our society, fear is erased because we can understand that the hearts of all people, if simply untwisted, have the desire to love unconditionally and do no harm to others.

By meditating upon the following principles, we can train ourselves to understand the values of our hearts and conscience over the false biases of society. The truths outlined here, even if they can't be comprehended on an intellectual level yet, should resonate strongly within, as each individual spirit recognizes authentic teachings of love and truth intuitively.

People who love God now are picturing a law giving ruler, sitting on a throne ready to judge humanity according to his commands. This is an untruth that has been keeping us locked in a mindset of darkness and ignorance. Let the truth shine in and heal our perceptions of God. God instead sits within each human.

Jesus taught that "according to thy faith be it unto you" (Matt 9:29). On the contrary, Old Testament thinking reflects "according to thy behavior shall it be unto you" and much of the world believes this way to this day. For instance, many believe that if bad things befall them, it could be because they did something displeasing to God. In this scenario God is in charge of a person's destiny and destiny is affected by one's behavior. On the other hand, according to Jesus, it is by one's intentions and beliefs that things occur to us.

Jesus often asked, "Do you believe?" before healing. If the answer was yes, the person was healed. But in the city where the people did not believe, Jesus could not heal. Matthew 13:58 is astounding if fully understood, "And he (Jesus) did not many mighty works there because of their unbelief." This supports the truth that a person has more authority over their circumstances than one knows. This should give us quite a novel perspective on cause and effect. Our beliefs affect our reality tremendously, and so it is intensely important to believe in the correct ideas.

The sages and shaman of ancient times described the ambiguous and incomprehensible essence of God as Spirit. The Bible States, "God is a Spirit" (John 4:24). Spirit was the name for that which was indefinable back then. Today we know the name for that which alludes to all the properties of God, and that thing is energy.

Through quantum theories, we have now determined that not only does energy explain all the properties of spirit, it has also been able to include the power of conscience within energy. It has been discovered that the field in which energy exists is consciousness. This is called the Unified Field theory of Consciousness. We already know that Jesus taught that conscience is the highest authority, the supreme ruler, the omnipresent god. Jesus and science proclaim the same truth.

Here is our new truth on the true image of God. There is one thing in this universe that has life giving power. There is one thing in this universe that is omnipresent. There is one thing in this universe that cannot be created or destroyed, thus it is eternal. This one thing is energy. Energy is God. But this energy is not void; it is filled with conscience. Jesus said he is in the Father, and the Father in him (John 10:38). If there is only one unified field of conscience energy in which everything exists, then in fact, everything is in God and God is in everything, which is the definition of an omnipresent god.

Conscience is within every human being, and therefore, the highest authority resides within the body. For this reason, we do not need outside governance. This needs to be our new perspective about God. He is not an external, far-away, life-directing, destiny-determining authority over the human. His power and love instead is within each individual human. Each person is the fullness of the omniscient god because his conscience is God. For this reason we need no protection from one another.

In the following paragraphs, we will analyze the shocking and transformative verses that support Jesus' lessons. We will examine each of these closely in the context of our new truth about God. These verses illuminate the power of God within. The ideas put forth here transcend what we have always believed about cause and effect, and god and man, but these reveal the true nature of the workings of our reality.

"Life and death are in the power of the tongue" (Proverbs 18:21). The very power of life and death (the ultimate power of God) is in the tongue of the human, says Proverbs 18. Our words are the words of God, and according to the energy behind our words, we can add positive energy to or pollute with negative energy. Our voice carries the energy of sound. This energy can be positive or negative depending upon the intention of our heart. If we mean to uplift, support and encourage, we add positive energy to the person we are directing our words toward. If we have malice in our hearts, even if our words are kind words, our intention shows through in the energy of our words, and we have the power to deflate another's energy or "kill" another's spirit. Each of us has heard of a person who has absolutely been made desolate and debilitated by verbal abuse.

"Thou shalt also decree a thing and it shall be established unto thee" (Job 22:28). This second verse comes from the ancient book of Job. It states that if a person declares something, that thing will be established. Again, this relates to the power of our voices, our words, and the intention behind our words. A simple example of this is when we profess something to children, and they believe wholeheartedly in what we have stated. We pronounce it, it is so. On the adult level, we have the power to establish something through the declaration of it. For instance, if you tell yourself you're a failure consistently, chances are that your prophecy will come true. In fact, Job says it is sure to come true. If you tell your partner time and again that they are beautiful with the conviction of a true heart behind your words, your partner is going to *feel* beautiful and *believe* they are beautiful, and then it is so, isn't it? For it is "according to our faith that it shall be" according to Jesus. Words are so very powerful, and this is why we have heard, "the Word is God."

This relates closely to our next verse from Hebrews 11, and this is the most amazing verse to scrutinize carefully. "Now faith is the substance of things hoped for, the evidence of things not seen" (Hebrews 11:1). Let us translate this parable in elementary terminology. What we believe and hope for becomes substance. What we believe in and hope for materializes. What materializes in your life is evidence of what you have been believing in your heart. Wow! This confirms what many new thinkers already believe, and that is that we create our own reality. Faith and belief are powerful energies of the mind that shall become substance.

Our thoughts and beliefs produce brain waves of measurable energy which can be recorded by EEG. If belief or faith or thoughts produce energy from the brain, and of course they do, then according to the Bible this energy will produce substance. Thus, the energy of our thoughts produce mass. This should sound familiar since Einstein proved that energy equals mass in his theory of relativity. If Einstein only knew that the Bible divulged this theory first.

"Therefore all things whatsoever ye would that men should do to you, do ye even so to them" (Matthew 7:12). This quote from Matthew 7 is where we get what is known as The Golden Rule. The saying basically suggests that we do unto others as we would have done unto us. Jesus encourages that whatever we would have happen to us, we should do that same unto others. This is because whatever we give out comes back to us. If we are negative toward others, we can receive that same negativity back in return from the energy field. It's as if giving out negative energy creates a void of negative energy within us, and therefore the universe rushes in to fill that void with more negative energy. In the same manner, if we emit positive energy and intention, the universe rushes in to fill us with more positive energy. This teaching reflects the system of karma in Eastern traditions. As the Bible teaches, one will reap as he sows.

The beauty of this enlightened knowledge is that when we have learned new truths, our personal energy changes. Our hearts and minds are renewed, rewired. We realize we are all one (united by the same conscience) and all good, and so never intend to harm another. We love our neighbor as ourselves because in reality, they are made of the exact substance we are made of. Remember, our goal in enlightenment is to renew our minds so we can be transformed. When we reprogram our minds, our minds are wired to the source, the light, the love as opposed to outside influences. Our hearts are filled with true love, not a feigned love which exists with prejudice and conditions upon behaviors, beliefs, and appearances.

To love in Hebrew means to give. At the point of true love, our hearts give out always a truly intended positive energy, and then that void will be filled with positive energy in return. When all we receive is positive energy from our surroundings, we are suddenly living in heaven. More on this later.

If all of these things stated in these verses are true, we are in control of our destiny. Some untouchable God out in the heavens is not determining the course of our life, but we are creating our own circumstances and our own reality. This is a hard concept to accept for many people for obvious reasons, but it is also a glorious one.

This leads us to our final verse where Jesus states to the scholars that their scriptures say "Ye are gods" (John 10:34). If we have the power over life and death, if what we decree becomes established, and if what we believe becomes substance, we are indeed gods. And so Jesus was the firstborn of many sons of God, says scripture (Romans 8:29), but this is only because he came to this enlightened realization very early on the timeline of evolution. We are God, all of us now in the flesh, Jesus being the first of many brethren. Collectively, through the same conscience energy which is present in us all and through our own god given power to create our own destinies, we are the body of the One Living God. We are the Creators. We are indeed gods.

Chapter 11

Awakening from the Dust

• • • •

Dear passengers, you may prepare for landing. We are now arriving at our destination in the glory land. After a lifetime of darkness and like a sleeping beauty, our souls can now stir and awaken. The time here is dawn. The sun is due to emerge on the horizon to shed light on that which has been cloaked in darkness. Our perceptions of the world have been dismantled and rearranged.

The eternal within us can take its proper place of honor here, rejoined by wisdom to our physical reality. With the merging of spiritual reality and physical illusion, we can now see that spirit energy usurps physical perception. It is the intention of the energy in our heart and mind that matters, and not our physical behavior or appearance. We are free to live in liberty by listening to our conscience, without restraint in our mannerisms or actions (because we can now trust our hearts to direct us into good behaviors only). With this newfound freedom, it's forever a new day here. We hope you have enjoyed your voyage.

When I resurrected and came out of the death and ignorance that law and religion had kept me in, I saw God face to face. He/she was a light that permeated every atom, every infinitesimal fiber of creation. This was an experience I had during one of my innumerable prayer and meditation sessions early one autumn morning. It was then that I realized many things about God, the nature of man, who God is, and the reason for existence.

First, I experienced to the depths of my soul the love of God. Though we now have a new image of God, his picture should saturated with the idea of love. There is a source of energy and light. That source is always giving forth the energy for life itself. The very propensity to be life giving includes the idea of profound love. God cannot give life unless God loves. Giving means loving. To give life is to love.

Secondly, God is conscious. Though God is not a man, God, the all-knowing, is conscious. We are deeply connected to him through our conscience, and he deeply connected to us. "He", God, is the part of us that we have not yet been able to open our minds to receive. He knows all, and though we have the ability to know all because we are him, there are still places of the brain that remain in darkness and things that we aren't cognizant of consciously yet. (God is, of course, genderless). God is available to us through deep meditation as our own conscious being. However, the more lights we turn on in the brain and the more connections we make to the truth, the closer we become to godliness.

Thirdly, the reason for being is to experience and record within our universal consciousness the experience of living as a flesh being. This is a topic too broad to expound upon here, but long story short, we incarnate in the flesh to experience the ultimate wonders and delights of a physical existence. We incarnate to love ourselves as one another, and one another as ourselves. As the volume of our recorded experiences grows, we grow closer to the ideal state of being, as physical beings acknowledging fully our spiritual nature. Essentially, we are here to love, to learn, and to move toward our ultimate hope, which is peace and harmony in the flesh. The first step in reconciling this is to experience our spiritual being as reigning over our physical being, and the energetic laws of the universe reigning over the physical laws of this world.

We know now that God is not a man (and scripture confirms this in Numbers 23:19), so why does all of Western society imagine him as beard wearing, silver haired, throne sitting man? The answer is that ancient patterns of belief are still pervasive in our thought processes. We have been primitive in our thinking and have held on, in our subconscious minds, to primal images of God. Now is the time to evolve our conscience by accepting new information which we began gathering decades, even centuries ago. Energy is real, the man in the sky is not, though they both have been able to reflect the exact same virtues: that of eternal power, that of omnipresence, that of omnipotence, even that of omniscience, as we now know through scientific studies.

This is called evolution of thought. As we evolve and learn more, our minds expand with more knowledge. Therefore to be close-minded is inherently against the flow of evolution and enlightenment and God. We, rather, support this evolution by remaining open minded and being able to accept new information.

The idea of a man sitting up in the sky, directing our every fate is an ancient notion, though it may have been effective for its era. While humanity was less informed, perhaps all we could conjure in our thinking to explain life and destiny was a man in the heavens controlling every action and deciding every fate on earth.

Man is evolving, and though religion might want to dispute this, the argument is futile. All one has to do is review history. Even modern history clearly reveals that men are getting smarter. We have gone from barbaric and crude behaviors and beliefs to a more civilized and peaceful society overall. Two thousand years ago, man did not know the earth was round. Man did not know the earth travelled around the sun, etc. History shows, through the death sentence for instance, that on a whim, life was expendable. Now we are more empathetic and have more respect for life, so much so that beheadings and hangings and executions and injections by governments are slowly becoming outlawed. This is a trend toward love, and love is God. Trending toward God is a journey toward ultimate intelligence.

There are just millions of facts that are simply a part of our knowing today, that were not known hundreds of years ago. Just a glimpse into the past century exhibits leaps and bounds in thought and information which we are constantly assimilating into our framework.

To become enlightened, we need to expand our knowledge, not limit it. Law directs the obedient to not do this, don't touch that, and don't mingle with someone outside of the group. Truth implores us to try it, experience it, learn from it, expand, grow, and live without the fear of judgment for doing so. If law is death, freedom from law is life. And that is what I came back to on my glorious resurrection day by the graces of the deep philosophical lessons of Jesus, which turn out to be contrary to the surface lessons of the Bible.

Through our faith in a foolish authority, we have believed that people need to conform to societal standards. Belief in the true authority allows for liberty to be different, unique, and diverse. When one realizes it is okay to express our own individual godliness in any way desired because that godliness is always inherently good, we live in heaven. On the contrary, imagine if every one of us became a purple pants wearing short haired yogi. To live in a place where everyone is uniform, cut to the same shape, size, and color by societal standards, is the definition of hell.

Enlightenment is a transformation in thinking that leads to a transformation in the heart and soul. Once we understand on an intellectual level that it is perfectly acceptable to allow people to express their own individuality, our hearts can become more accepting of the strange and diverse customs of other cultures and traditions. These unique flavors add color to our garden. Once we realize the truth, that each person is truly good at heart, made of the same godly conscience as us (regardless of their current behavior), there is nothing to fear in others. In having the awareness that conformity is not required, we are free to love all equally, no matter how they look, what they believe, or how they choose to live. Having no prejudice equates to assessing life through pure unqualified knowledge, and obtaining that is at the root of what enlightenment is.

The fact is all people are in a bit of darkness because of the principles we live by and the religion we practice every day through law. It turns out that this lack of knowledge is a perfectly valid and the only acceptable excuse for bad behavior, especially when incorrect information is all one has ever lived by. When a person has been taught to listen to a false authority, rather than to listen to his intuitive authority, how can he be blamed for thinking unnaturally, and thereby acting unnaturally? In understanding these principles of enlightenment, we become able to *forgive* all ignorant behaviors as Jesus forgives.

Whereas many of us look at the world today with negativity and pessimism, enlightenment gives us hope. Our hope is explained in this way: Man is evolving, therefore man is getting smarter and learning more truth. As man becomes more enlightened, his heart expands to be more accepting and as a result more loving, as just explained above. By the process of evolution, all will be less limited by false standards. All will become more understanding, more forgiving, and more accepting, and this is a trend toward the unconditional love of God. The truth of our conscience shines through more and more each day. Our conscience is good, our conscience is light, and the more we listen to this intuition within ourselves, the more the darkness on this earth will vanish.

Those who are yet closed-minded say that the state of morality in the world seems to be getting worse. This is contrary to evolution, however, and is not true. Overall, the state of morality is improving, as we see in a united move toward more integration and greater acceptance. The goal is for eventual freedom for all. No limitations, no conditions, no boundaries, no country, no exclusive groups, just loving every neighbor as ourselves. The virtue of loving everyone as ourselves has a direct consequence of doing no harm to another. Thus, no need for government.

When one's prejudices have been washed away by truth, the heart opens and begins to love without hypocrisy. A true love is gained through truth, and in that, one can't help but rejoice at the lack of burden that forgiveness and acceptance brings. Unconditional and unbiased love for all erases fear. (As the Bible says, perfect love casts out fear in 1 John 4:18). With the realization that we are all part of a greater whole, comes the desire to help, support and encourage all. If I instead harm another, I harm the whole, of which I am included.

To walk in a place where we have love and respect for everything we see, as everything is in us and us in everything, is to walk in paradise. This garden, with all its diversity, color, pleasures, and delights flourishes in the light of truth. I see God everywhere I look because God *is* everywhere I look, and that is the very definition of living in heaven. I have found the Kingdom of God which lies within, and that Kingdom manifests without now.

The truth that everybody understands but has a hard time applying is that to manifest heaven on earth, we have to start by changing the landscape within. We transform the landscape within by acquiring a new truth, the real truth. When we believe in the true principles that govern the spiritual world, we have hope, for it is only love that rules and forever gives and shines eternally. The spiritual energetic world is where the truth is. The principles of love, growth, acceptance, and harmony are what rule in the heavens. The physical may still be ruled by law, but the spiritual trumps the carnal as we are all spiritual beings first and foremost.

As we arrive at our destination at the end of our journey, the Bible speaks of a new heaven and a new earth. I want to welcome you to both. By now, your image of heaven should have changed. There should no longer be a tyrant sitting in the throne of our heaven who loves conditionally, but we shall have come to conquer that enemy to replace him with a big heart of loving life-giving energy.

Earth should take on a new visage for us also in the light of truth.

Earth is an intricate part of the god that we are, for we cannot live in the absence of her nourishment, her fruit, her balance, her beauty. No longer should we see a sea of evil and criminal sinners when we look around us. We should see our unconventional, mismatched, and downright eccentric family members, and appreciate what an interesting melodious harmony we all create together. This earth is the beautiful diverse and colorful garden we have created to enjoy forever. Knowing that God forgives all physical acts because they are simply due to ignorance and detachment from intuition, perhaps we can forgive all too.

In enlightenment, prejudice is erased from the mind. God doesn't judge us by our deeds, how can man judge another man by his behaviors? God judges the heart. The glory of that is deep within every man's heart is the truth of love. Thus, we are all judged equally as good. And so you are "forgiven" teaches the Bible, but in actuality you were never guilty in the first place. It is only law which has deceived us into believing we could be guilty in the eyes of God. Not true. God gave us all the same heart, made of the same substance of purity and innocence, and our physical behaviors simply don't matter. As God loves us, how can we not love one another with a profound and unconditional love?

Chapter 12

At Home with Enlightenment

• • • •

We have made it through our desert wilderness, and we have now arrived in the Promised Land. Jesus stated in Matthew 18:3, "Except ye be converted, and become as little children, ye shall not enter into the kingdom of heaven." Children have an unconditional love until they are taught to be prejudice. Innocence and trust is our first state of being. Where this purity flourishes should feel like home to us, for it is our natural essence. We were born without prejudice and ignorance, in the likeness of God, and enlightenment brings us back from the defiled state we fell to by eating from the knowledge of good and evil (through living under law).

The Bible now becomes the most magical if not ironic fairy tale ever written. Though it is true in every sense of the word, the religion formed from the Bible is not the Truth. Though I needed the guidance of the governing system of the Bible to get me through the valley of the shadow of death, government is not the Way. Though following the law of the Bible promises life, it does not disclose that it first brings death, and it leaves most but a few in its deep dark grave. The Bible calls itself allegory, and Jesus only spoke in parables, but we have now decoded the riddle.

The Bible mirrors life. We live under government as did all the

Israelites. The attempt to always serve and sacrifice for God put the people in a state of bondage and death in a dry desert wilderness. They ignorantly believed that people were not worthy of love if they misbehaved in the physical form. They developed prejudices against sinners and others from outside their community, as do we today. In the end, Jesus was supposed to save us all from that tyranny and the incorrect belief patterns produced by the system, and set us free to love unconditionally. We have completely missed the hidden teachings of Messiah, though he has walked among us for two millennia.

The principles of the book of law are corrupt, even though the book teaches the actual truth in a coded message. Few have been able to decipher the puzzle for the true message, and you are now one of those few. That ancient and enigmatic communication could not be simpler now that we have found the light: Inside Every Human Heart is the Throne of GOD. We, as one organism united are God. For any human to rule over another is the cause for criminal tendencies, prejudice, limited thinking, and stunted growth, all of which are contrary to human nature. Therefore pain, suffering and oppression abound.

The irony is that once one emerges from belief in the ignorant principles that government imposes, one discovers that civil governance is not the true way of God, but written in the heart only is the true way of God. Though once enlightened, a person will leave religion (as it is founded on false principles), it could be a necessary stepping stone on the journey to enlightenment.

What we are freed from now is religion and its god who governs by rules and oppression. Unfortunately, in life, we still have to live by the rules and standards of government and society, and there is nothing we can do to escape that reality for now.

An enlightened person can still witness and feel that pain and sorrow that surrounds us on a daily basis in the physical realm. Luckily through enlightenment, there is a tremendous difference in our perspective of this suffering.

When one believes in the standards put forth by this society, one develops a personal identity which is shaped by those standards. That personal identity is perceived as a separate entity from all other individuals and is known as the ego. The ego's job is to protect the identity from the fear put forth by this judgment based world.

When one realizes through the truth of enlightenment that one's true identity is the omnipresent limitless loving *I am*, one can erase the ego, for there truly is nothing to protect the self from. The true self is one with everything. A person can now not be offended, for there are no personal boundaries for any stranger to cross in the unity and oneness of all things. This is a very deep and transformative truth.

I hear the arguments from my readers stating that they would defend themselves and would never let another confront or offend them. But this is the ego speaking, not the true character of the godliness within. We forget the lesson of Christ, who was powerful enough to stop any assault, yet died passively as a martyr to the system. Jesus, 'til death did not fight, though he was never in the wrong.

There is one reason that Jesus did not defend himself. There is one reason why Jesus said even about his executioners "Forgive them Father, for they know not what they do." Here it is: There are not two sides, a good versus an evil, but only one side. Who is there to fight against when you are one with all? Jesus showed no display of ego, only the higher truth that we do unto others as we would have done unto us.

There are energies at play behind the scenes of this physical reality, and when one argues, struggles, fights, and competes, it adds to the energy of conflict. Jesus taught us to turn the other cheek because he knew that fighting only adds to violence. Fighting adds to the energy of war. Resistance of any kind in the energetic level hampers the flow of the positive. In fighting and resistance then, peace cannot be accomplished.

When one peacefully accepts the outside reality, but defers to the inner truth instead where there is always unity, one can let go of any dilemma. In releasing the stressful realities of the physical realm, we automatically attune with the truth adding our god given energy to the harmony that flows behind the scenes. There is nothing to fear, and nothing to fight. The will of God, which is for harmony and peace for all, will win someday. We can start by being this change – always peaceful, always trusting, and accepting of everyone no matter their physical behavior or custom.

We are one with all in the spiritual reality, for there is nothing else in the universe but conscious living energy. The illusion of duality comes from the knowledge of two sides, the knowledge of good and evil. There is no evil in the reality of truth, if all that exists is part of the living loving whole. In this way, the devil is destroyed. He's just a ghost, an illusion, a delusion. As discussed before, evil is an act that is performed by a twisted mind. At birth, all minds are pure and straight until the structures of society begin to confuse and mislead. There is not evil at work, but ignorance.

Therefore to help the progression of the light, we must stop fighting on every level. People are not our enemies, they are just lacking truth and believing in false principles. Though we can shine a light on the truth and be a beacon of compassion, though we can plant seeds for harmony, we can't stand against the perceived injustices of the world. Though society may appear to be going to the dogs in the physical, behind the curtain, evolution is not moving backwards toward ruin and destruction. We know that Great God is only and forever giving forth more light, more love, and more positivity, and God wins this battle because he is omnipotence defined.

To stand against something is not to be for the opposite. To stand against something only creates more negativity that hurts both sides. Instead we always stand with something, never against. The only thing to stand with is the side of passivity, acceptance, and love for all, as Jesus would. Usually if that side is true, it is not participating in the battle but observing it trustingly only, not in the turbulence of battle, but on the shore as a lighthouse.

The observer behind the ego is witness to much chaos, recognizing that chaos is a product of untruths. Untruths are lies and the definition of a lie is something that does not exist, therefore there is nothing to fight. Thus, evil does not truly exist though we seem to witness it in this world. Scriptures state that Jesus defeated the devil and his works, and this was accomplished by shining the light and exposing the lies of our belief systems. There is nothing to fight in the presence of all-encompassing goodness. We are to trust in the victorious power of the greatest energy of all and simply shine a light of truth.

To bring peace into our reality, we simply need to set our intentions for peace. We have to believe in the overarching unity and harmony that exists in the spiritual realm by belief in the power that is only and always flowing with harmony. For instance, if everyone on planet earth could focus on peace, acceptance, love, compassion and harmony for one day, just one day - what would that day look like? Heaven, we will have attained heaven on earth for those 24 hours. Even if all peoples could attain this peace for just a day, that peace could not last at this juncture because ego, fear, and false beliefs are still the basis for the foundations of our physical world. For everlasting peace, one needs to journey to the truth within, transform his thoughts on a deep level, and then always focus on peace for all days. When every human begins to see the light by obtaining more knowledge, peace will come to the individual heart and then finally to the outer world.

Fortunately, once enlightened, one cannot go back. All the pathways in the mind have been renewed and rewired to Truth, to the Source, to the Light. The love in the heart cannot be erased, tainted, nor even damaged, for there is nothing in this physical world that can upset the truth of the truer spiritual world. Ironically, it is the spiritual world which is the truth, and the physical which is the illusion as quantum physics proves, is it not? If all were to open their hearts to the greater truth, we would then have peace. Earth would then transfigure into a beautiful garden, not only on the spiritual plane, but on the physical too.

Despite the fact that we are left living in two worlds, nothing should be able to shake the hope we have in our hearts that man will outsmart all the world's problems. In one world, the spiritual and energetic world, we can have absolute peace and trust in the progress of the Great Energy of God which is always moving forward with light and love. The energy is so powerful, it will not be denied its purpose. Its truth will not remain hidden as more and more people awaken through evolution of thought. The lights are constantly being turned on as people grow in wisdom and compassion. That light cannot be extinguished or buried.

In this paradise, we can have full and unconditional love for all conscious beings, so much so that we should not harm man nor animal. Even animals are part of the conscious One. They are me, and I am them, and we are fueled by the same loving light within. As Leonardo Da Vinci once stated "The time will come when men such as I look upon the murder of animals as they now look on the murder of men." Recognizing that compassion is the only way for all beings is part of enlightenment. Knowing this similar heart we all share for compassion and love for all living things is complete and utter freedom. We may mask or twist this compassion now, but on a profound level, we all desire compassion and peace. We cannot stand for, nor could we perform, the harming of another conscious being, let alone commit its slaughter. *We must practice without hypocrisy,* "Do unto others."

Our spiritual garden can include an infallible hope for mankind and the destiny of our race. We will grow in love as the limitations of falsehoods dissipate. We are fated to grow in wisdom and acceptance as we realize we are limitless beings living in an abundant universe. As man awakens to his intuitive power and his innate love, we are bound for joy and glory.

In the spirit, there can be less pain and suffering in knowing that we are one with all, and humanity is evolving. Evolution of the mind and heart leads to enlightenment. With more light in our conscience, we are closer to God and so less and less harm will be done. Humanity will arrive at greater peace someday. This is inevitable, and the goal of evolution.

These truths may sound too idealistic to some. Remember however, you are a spiritual being first. Thus, the laws that dictate the physical world are subject to the spiritual and energetic laws. The laws of energy work like the principles of karma: reap as you sow, do unto others, believe a thing for it to be true. Ultimately, we as individuals are capable of creating a perfect and harmonious sanctuary called Earth. These are the truths of the spirit realm.

After taking this journey, we are supposed to be thinking differently than we thought at the time we opened this book to begin reading. You must believe in new principles and new pathways if you are to experience the truth of enlightenment.

This has been an intellectual and philosophical map to the source of light within. Some people will still need an emotional map or have the need to follow their own treasure map to the pearl within. If you have had a hard time assimilating this information, you must go to your heart and conscience. Find that lost and hidden path inside. It is there waiting for you to seek it.

Dare to travel back to the garden from which we fell so long ago by the false knowledge of laws, division, prejudice and standards. Come instead to the knowledge of the spirit realm where no one needs to be governed and no one is judged. Like a child, you are innocent and pure. Though you have been taught that the gates are closed to the homeland, and a monster guards the entrance, that enemy is simply an illusion, a shadow, a lie made real by faulty belief systems. Knowing that that enemy's house stands on sand in the midst of a whirlwind extinguishes his power. His foundation of law is worthless and soon to pass away. The only truth at the end of the pathway is harmony, peace, and love. I tell you truly, God waits there for you with open arms, longing for you to come home.

Other books by Rev. Anna Grace can be found Amazon.com or at:
www.createspace.com/6588574 Baptism: The Journey Into Death
www.createspace.com/6208778 Jesus Law
www.createspace.com/6223890 So You Think You Know Jesus
www.createspace.com/6229631 Where the Devil Hides
www.createspace.com/6182850 Gay: What Does the Bible Really Say?
www.createspace.com/5286560 An Alternative Apocalypse

JESUS LAW

Many have never known Jesus as one to get involved in law or politics. For many, he was simply the victim of an unjust system gone wrong, sentenced to death though innocent. How could the legislation of the day justify this act of murder? Perhaps there was a flaw in the system. Perhaps Jesus has more to say about this legal system than most realize.

Revealed in the pages of this book is the truth of the wisdom of Jesus Christ. Jesus' beliefs about law are deeply philosophical and fundamentally radical, though not many are ever exposed to this portion of Jesus' doctrine. The mystery of Jesus as more than just a King from another world, but a master of the ways of this world also, are hidden in parable in scripture. Jesus is one who had completely studied law and legislation, one who was able to astonish the lawyers and judges even as a child. But what was this ideology which ultimately would lead the way to truth, freedom, liberty, and justice for all?

Discover the mysteries of the fascinating and brilliant mind that was Jesus Christ, and be transformed by the renewing of your mind. Be prepared to change your beliefs through the knowledge that few have been able to assimilate.

SO YOU THINK YOU KNOW JESUS

The Lord and Savior, King of Heaven and soon to be King of this World, Jesus Christ is a persona that many of us think we know.

His name and face are one of the most recognized on planet earth, and for good reason. He is the main character of the best-selling book of all time. However, there wouldn't be much of a story here if those who claimed incontestably to know Jesus actually knew Jesus. In fact, scripture says we simply cannot know Jesus in full until he is fully revealed on that glorious day. Be prepared to be astonished as you come to know the full truth behind the character of Jesus. The author presents irrefutable proof that Jesus is nothing like we imagine him to be. Ready yourself to see Jesus as he truly appears in his full glory. Few. Few, says scripture, will be privy to this revelation.

GAY: What does the Bible really say?
Perhaps you have read others books on what the Bible says about Homosexuality. Perhaps you have read the books that argue that scriptures have been translated wrong. This book does not bow out with cowardly excuses. Perhaps you have read books that argue that according to scripture homosexuality is unclean, but it is not defined as an actual 'sin,' and so it is okay. This is faulty reasoning and simply nothing more than word play. This book is different.

There is no wordplay here, there is no loose interpretation, there is no skirting around the issue. All that is presented here is a head on, take the bull by the horns truth. There simply is no way to argue this philosophy, for it is nothing but scriptural proof which cannot be argued away. Even the most learned Bible scholar cannot dismiss the undeniable fundamental principle which is presented within these pages. An astonishing revelation of irrefutable, life-changing, mind-transforming truth.

Most of society knows that the Bible states that for a man to lie with another man is an abomination to God, for it is written boldly in black and white. But did you know that there are several other scriptures in which the Bible speaks of homosexual law? You have not heard these quoted in social circles or churches, and the truth of them is shocking. In this radical revelation of truth, the author shows exactly how and why our current perceptions regarding sexual orientation is not cohesive with God's true sentiment about homosexuality. The mystery of God's opinion will be revealed and proven through the examination of little known and hidden concepts. This dynamic book takes a new look at Biblical scripture to set us free from the delusions of erroneous principles and doctrines. A must read for all who are or know a gay person. A revolutionary doctrine that will change fundamental ideologies. Rest assured, God is not against gays, even though the Bible says very clearly and callously, "For a man to lie with another man is an abomination." Find out how this oxymoron is true.

WHERE THE DEVIL HIDES
A deep philosophical discourse on the nature of civilization
The Bible uses many riddles, parables, and symbols to tell a hidden story that is cloaked mysteriously beneath the visible black and white letters. One theme that is seen repeatedly in scripture is the serpent wrapped around a tree, a piece of wood or a pole. The devil, or Lucifer, or Satan as he is known was also a serpent in the Garden of Eden who is depicted as twisted around the tree of knowledge. Again this same emblem is found in Numbers 21 when Moses lifted up a serpent upon a pole before the Israelites. Exodus 4 produces this serpent again when Moses first acquired his powerful walking staff, which was originally a wooden pole which turned into a serpent. How could these three appearances of the serpent on a wooden stick be related? What clues are being given through this symbol? What is the serpent doing in the hand of Moses, and what is the hidden agenda of the devil running deep within the roots of the scriptures? The devil's agenda will be revealed as he is pulled out of the secrecy of the shadows and exposed in the brightness of truth. The devil has never been revealed in this way. Once his mask is removed, his face is

very familiar. The reality of the matter is absolutely shocking. Come discover what few ever dig deeply enough to find.

BAPTISM: THE JOURNEY INTO DEATH

There are untold truths about the act of baptism. Your church may explain baptism to you, but what does the Bible actually say about being baptized into the Christian religion?

The doctrine of baptism which we hold to be true in our minds is a complete fallacy, according to the Bible itself. Our beliefs about our baptisms are not founded on Biblical Scripture.

The Bible says that when we make our commitment to follow this religion by the act of baptism, we get buried with Christ into his death and ours. We are buried and also die. We are baptized and enter death. This is the scriptural truth of baptism. Baptism causes death. Find out just what your death entails, why you are buried with Christ by baptism, and how to escape your grave.

AN ALTERNATIVE APOCALYPSE

Lo Here! Lo There! Are you looking for the return of the visible Christ according to the signs of the times and the wars and rumors of wars in the world? In this past century, end-time prophetic events have been fulfilled on our earth like never before. Armies today surround Israel. The 20th century also brought us a tremendous prophetic fulfillment when Israel returned to its homeland. There were two world wars fought, and at this very moment there are many foreboding skirmishes in and around the Holy Land. Many have arisen in remote corners of the world professing to be the Christ. According to scripture, all of these are great apocalyptic foreshadows to alert us to the possibility, even the probability, that we are in the last days.

At this crucial point in history, there is something we must consider. Is it possible that as Israel was misled by strict scriptural interpretation under the Old Covenant, so today is Christianity misled in the same way, and that is why we, too, believe that the second advent of Messiah will be as a conquering King? If we are waiting for Messiah King Jesus to come and destroy all wickedness and evil and save all of humanity, is it possible that we may have fallen into the same doctrinal error as the old religious sect in Jesus' day? They, back then, missed the mark by a long shot. There is nothing new under the sun, and just as it was historically at his first coming, it seems that we may today be in the same mindset, and therefore not prepared for his second coming. It may be time to look at eschatological scripture anew.

About the Author

Anna is a wife and mother of two. She is an Ordained Minister and has earned her Masters in Metaphysics. She has been on a tremendous spiritual journey over the past several years of her life and has devoted herself to meditation, study, investigation, and research into that which we call God. Her philosophical perspectives are as novel as they are profound. Anna has been able to decode many spiritual mysteries that have moved her understanding far beyond the realm of religion and into the new paradigm of Enlightenment. Now she writes to help others understand life from a new perspective. Life is so much more glorious than what it appears to be in our reality.

As an author, Anna writes about the untold mysteries of the Bible, not only as a religious text, but also as an ethical, legal, and philosophical document. Though rarely explored, the Bible has profound theories on the nature of humanity, the course and role of legislation in civilization, and the problem of religion, which are deeply concealed within parable. Her goal is to bring these obscure truths to light in order that individuals can contemplate and meditate on these cutting edge concepts which are not normally taught in religious environments.

Printed in the United States
By Bookmasters